CLARENDON'S
FOUR PORTRAITS

CLARENDON'S FOUR PORTRAITS

George Digby: John Berkeley
Henry Jermyn: Henry Bennet

From the supplement to the
Clarendon State Papers vol. iii (1786)

edited with an
introduction and notes

by

RICHARD OLLARD

HAMISH HAMILTON · LONDON

HAMISH HAMILTON LTD

Published by the Penguin Group
27 Wrights Lane, London W8 5TZ, England
Viking Penguin Inc, 40 West 23rd Street, New York, New York 10010, U.S.A.
Penguin Books Australia Ltd, Ringwood, Victoria, Australia
Penguin Books Canada Ltd, 2801 John Street, Markham, Ontario, Canada L3R 1B4
Penguin Books (N.Z.) Ltd, 182–190 Wairau Road, Auckland 10, New Zealand

Penguin Books Ltd, Registered Offices: Harmondsworth, Middlesex, England

First published in Great Britain 1989 by
Hamish Hamilton Ltd

Introduction, footnotes etc. copyright © 1989 by Richard Ollard

1 3 5 7 9 10 8 6 4 2

British Library Cataloguing in Publication Data
Ollard, Richard, 1923–
Clarendon portraits.
1. England. Politics. Clarendon, Edward Hyde.–Earl of
I. Title
942.06′092′4

ISBN 0-241-12632-0

Typeset by Goodfellow & Egan, Cambridge
Printed by Butler and Tanner Ltd,
Frome and London

To John Grigg and Kenneth Rose

who share Clarendon's gifts
for friendship and for biography

LIST OF ILLUSTRATIONS

ACKNOWLEDGMENTS

I am grateful to the Delegates of the Clarendon Press for permission to reprint the text of these biographical studies from the supplement to vol iii of the Clarendon State Papers (1786) and to the Curators of the Bodleian Library for allowing me to collate it with the manuscript in their possession.

I also wish to express my thanks to the owners of the pictures, whose permission to reproduce is acknowledged in the list of illustrations. I regret that I have not been able to reproduce a portrait of a young man at Sherborne Castle, traditionally said to be the 1st Earl of Bristol, an identification which on grounds of costume, likeness or the age of the sitter can hardly be sustained. It has been suggested by Sir Oliver Millar that this intelligent-looking, fair-haired young man is in fact George Digby, the future 2nd Earl. Sir Oliver Millar tentatively attributes the portrait to Johann Priwitzer, who painted in 1627 a set of portraits of the children of the 4th Earl of Bedford, including a full-length of Digby's future brother-in-law, William, Lord Russell, his fellow-sitter in the great Van Dyck at Althorp.

Richard Ollard

LIST OF ABBREVIATIONS

B.L.	British Library
Cal. Clar. S.P.	*Calendar of the Clarendon State Papers*
Cal. S.P. Dom.	*Calendar of State Papers Domestic*
Clar. MS	Clarendon Manuscript
Clar. S.P.	*Clarendon State Papers*
Cont.	*Continuation of the Life written by himself*
D.N.B.	*Dictionary of National Biography*
Hist.	*The History of the Rebellion and Civil Wars in England*
Thurloe S.P.	*Thurloe State Papers*

INTRODUCTION

No aspect of Clarendon's career is more striking than his use of adversity. It was when he was a proscribed but insignificant exile in Jersey after the first Civil War, excluded even from the counsels of the émigré court of the Prince of Wales, that he wrote the first seven books of the *History of the Rebellion*. Twenty years later, once again and far more dispiritingly an exile, he turned the desert of experience into a garden of the Muses. Old, ill, bereaved, disgraced, ruined and solitary, he kept his head, his faith and his nerve. It was not for nothing that he had made a special study of the Psalms. Who has better exemplified the image of 'such as going through the vale of misery use it for a well and the pools are filled with water'?

In his second and last exile Clarendon's first concern was, naturally enough, to clear his name from the accusations that had been brought against him. *The Vindication of Myself* was begun in July 1668. Simultaneously he embarked on an autobiography, *the Life written by himself*. This work, which he subsequently used as a quarry for the extended and amplified *History of the Rebellion*, gave him full scope for the exercise of his gifts as a portraitist. He had shown himself (so far as we know he was his only reader) what he could do in the *History* written in 1647–8. But in the twenty years' interval his powers had matured. His experience of men and affairs had increased beyond measure. He knew what it was to hold the highest office, to manage, or attempt to manage, a party in Parliament, to deal with European statesmen first as a poor relation representing a penniless King in exile and then after 1660 as an equal. That he was thereby better equipped to be the historian of his times he was certain: 'There never yet was a good history written but by men conversant in affairs'. And it was as a history of his times that he wrote his autobiography. Childhood and youth, so often the most vivid, most sharply focused scenes in a man's account of his life, are scarcely touched on. Private emotions, personal pleasures, the fears and hopes of awakening ambition are excluded, except where a taste or a friendship can be shown to have helped to form the public character of the author. Alone of his family his father is brought into the centre of the stage. His mother, who survived her husband by nearly thirty years, is formally complimented and dismissed in half a sentence. His partner in a long and happy marriage whose death, some thought, had been caused by grief and anxiety on his behalf earns a more heartfelt but not a longer mention. Of the children in whom he took such pride and pleasure only his daughter makes a personal appearance – and that only because her secret marriage to the heir to the throne was itself a political fact of the first importance.

The *Life* in fact is, and was from the start intended to be, a history. Its tone and its perspective differ from the work begun in Jersey. Its author was older, infinitely more experienced, and, to a degree that few could have borne, his own man. He was not, as he had been twenty years earlier, writing for the King in order that mistakes could be analysed and wiser policies framed. He could not, as he had then, call upon colleagues to produce first-hand evidence of affairs he had had no hand in or documents to refresh his memory of those in which he had. The perspective, the purpose and the materials had all changed. But Clarendon's reading of history in both the literal and metaphorical sense had not. All those years ago in Jersey he had prepared himself for his task by reading Livy, Tacitus and Thucydides. In Montpellier they were his models still. The delineation of character, the representation of individuals in action and in argument, 'making the reader present at all they say and do', was the hallmark of good history.

The harvest of his activity has long been gathered into the great works, so much admired, so often impugned, so infrequently reprinted.[1] But some considerable gleanings have lain almost unnoticed and only with difficulty accessible in the supplement to the third volume of the Clarendon State Papers published in 1786. These are the Characters here reprinted.

In the original edition they appear, under the single word 'Characters', as those of Lord Digby, Sir John Berkeley and Sir Henry Bennet. But in an article written in 1973[2] Mr Graham Roebuck pointed out that the opening paragraph of the character of Bennet is really an entirely separate study of someone else. Quite apart from the sense of the text a glance at the manuscript from which it was printed at once confirms the observation. The passage is written on a self-contained folio and verso. Both it and the character of Bennet that follows begin on a fresh sheet with an initial capital 'H' for 'He' as do those of Digby and Berkeley. The mistake must be that of the eighteenth-century editor, Thomas Monkhouse, since it is in his hand that the heading 'Sir Henry Bennet' is superscribed over this piece.

The manuscript in question, Bodleian Library Clarendon MS 122, is in a clear copyist's hand, presumably that of Clarendon's secretary, William Shaw, since the first leaf bears the inscription in Clarendon's own hand, 'Mountpelier Apr 1669' and the first character, that of Digby, contains autograph alterations and insertions by the author. The date

---

[1] The most recent edition of the *Life*, itself an unsatisfactory one, is that of 1857. As long ago as 1909 Sir Charles Firth, as Regius Professor of Modern History, publicly called on the University Press to commission another.

[2] *Notes and Queries* 20, 168–170.

and provenance of the copy from which the Oxford edition was printed are thus clearly established.

Who is the fourth character briefly intruded between Berkeley and Arlington (to use the title by which Bennet is better known)? His discoverer suggests George Villiers, second Duke of Buckingham. I think Henry Jermyn, first Earl of St Albans, fits such specifications as there are somewhat more closely. The portrait, it must be said, is not one of Clarendon's more distinguished performances. Short on particularities it is long on censure. If the sitter were as deplorable a figure as is represented, the reader surely deserves, needs, a more circumstantial account. To say that he 'did more mischief than any man of the age he lived in, being the occasion of more prejudice to the King and to the Crown than any man of his condition ever was, and took more pains to lessen the King's reputation, and to make his person undervalued, than any other man did; and all this without the least purpose of infidelity, or desire of abating his prerogative, which he wished should be as high as any King's ever was, and desired only that they might prevail over it over whom he could prevail, and in that regard he cared not how low his reputation came to be' is to stake a claim for the man's historical importance, however shallow and trivial a person he might be in himself. Why and how, one wants to know, did he come to do such damage? And why does not Clarendon tell us?

A clue to both problems is given in the opening and closing phrases of the piece. 'He was a man bred from his cradle in the Court, and had no other business in the world than to be a good Courtier.' That narrows the field. The context of the passage quoted in the preceding paragraph makes it clear that the King referred to must be Charles I not Charles II. Both Charles I and his Queen had such an instinct for choosing disastrous favourites that a crop of names suggest themselves, Will Murray leading by a clear length. But the closing phrase gives him and a number of others their quietus: ' . . . if he dies without some very signal calamity, he may well be looked upon as a man of rare felicity.' The sitter evidently was still alive in 1669. Will Murray had died in 1651.

But Jermyn had not. Jermyn was indestructible. Clarendon had first come across him before he himself had entered the King's service and Jermyn, even then, was an established courtier. It was in 1633 when the young Mr Hyde, still grieving for the loss of his first wife in the previous year and still living much in her family circle, was called on by her cousin, Lord Grandison, for support in a scandal that threatened their name. Grandison's sister, Eleanor Villiers, a maid of honour to the Queen, had been seduced by Jermyn under promise of marriage from which he subsequently drew back. Grandison, informed by his sister of her pregnancy and its circumstances, issued a challenge. The King, warned of a duel between persons so intimately connected with the Crown, clapped them both in the Tower. It was at that point that Mr Hyde volunteered to negotiate a settlement on Grandison's behalf. This should have been easy. The King had made Jermyn's release conditional on his honouring the promise of marriage which would have satisfied the Villiers family. But the force of the phrase just quoted now becomes apparent: 'he desired only that they might prevail over it [the King's prerogative] over whom he could prevail'. Jermyn had early established an ascendancy in the favour of Henrietta Maria, which he never lost. Indeed in her widowhood it was widely rumoured that he became her lover, some even say her secret husband. Not for the last time she nullified the counsel of Mr Hyde by persuading Charles I to go back on his better judgment. Jermyn was released, dismissed nominally into a brief exile, only to be again received at Court and, in 1639, appointed Master of the Horse to the Queen. The King refused to receive a petition from the Villiers family, perhaps betraying a troubled conscience by his angry assertion that he knew more about the affair than they did, more than it was fit for them to know.

All this is clear enough from a number of sources, including the letters that Clarendon wrote to his father at the time.[3] What had brought it all back to him in 1669 was the writing of his autobiography. Here he retells 'this particular little story, in itself of no seeming consequence' because it was the cause of his first becoming known at Court. The acquaintance he then formed '. . . the friends and enemies he then made, had an influence upon the whole course of his life afterwards'.[4] But although he mentions the name of Lord Grandison he does not identify anyone else; indeed he makes a point of not doing so: 'nor shall their names ever come upon the stage by any record of mine'. Not only Jermyn, but Henrietta Maria was still alive when he was writing.[5] That would help to explain the elaborate circumlocution by which he camouflages Jermyn's place in her affections and the leverage thus given him over Charles I.

There are other clues that point to Jermyn, in particular the attention drawn to his self-indulgence in matters of food and drink and to his passion for gambling, 'the spunge that sucked in, and the gulph that swallowed up all he could get'. Jermyn was not singular in these tastes among Stuart courtiers. But his overmastering passion for play was conspicuous even in the looser world of Charles II. John Evelyn's sketch of him in extreme old age when he was too blind to see his food strikingly confirms Clarendon's description.

It is incredible how easy a life this Gent: has lived, and in what plenty even abroad, whilst his Majestie was a sufferer; nor lesse, the immense summs he has lost at play, which yet at about 80 yeares old he continues, having one that sets by him to name the spot in the Chards: He eate & dranke with extraordinary appetite. He is with all this a prudent old Courtier, & much inrich'd since his Majestie's returne.[6]

[3] B.L. Add. MS 4187 ff. 28 ff.

[4] Life I, 13–14.

[5] She died at her château of Colombes, near Paris, at the end of August 1669.

[6] Diary ed. de Beer iv, 337–8, 18 Sept 1683.

Evelyn, like Clarendon, had been in Paris in the early 1650s and had been shocked by 'the plenty and pomp' in which Jermyn had lived 'whilst the greatest and best men were exercised with all kinds of adversity'.[7] It is noteworthy too that Evelyn saw Jermyn as a man who had made a handsome living simply out of being a courtier. Finally Clarendon's statement that 'he had lived above forty years at the expense of the Crown' tallies exactly with Jermyn's appointment as a Vice-Chamberlain to the Queen on 2 July 1628.[8]

If therefore we accept Jermyn as the fourth member of the quartet along with Digby, Jack Berkeley and Arlington, does the conjunction suggest any general idea or were these studies discarded for reasons which bear no relation to each other? Only Clarendon himself could answer the question, but the asking of it may yield some insight into their particular qualities. The first and most obvious connection is that all four were personal not merely political enemies who had triumphed at his fall. Jermyn had been out of the country on a special embassy to Paris at the time, but this had enabled him, as Clarendon bitterly recalled in the *Life*, to make the early part of his exile even bleaker than it need have been. Of the others Berkeley had borne a private grudge against Clarendon since the time they were exiles in the early 1650s, Digby had actually attempted to impeach the Chancellor of High Treason in 1663, and Arlington was by all accounts the prime mover in his overthrow and, three months later, in persuading the King to force him into exile.[9] They were all men who would come at once to mind when Clarendon was thinking about his vindication.

A further point in common was that they all belonged to the generation that had come to manhood before the Civil War. Jermyn was perhaps half a dozen years older than

---

[7] Clarendon's own expression in the Character see p. 127.

[8] See Firth's article in the *D.N.B.* Graham Roebuck's candidate, the second Duke of Buckingham, was then a baby of six months and heir to a vast fortune.

[9] Violet Barbour, *Henry Bennet, Earl of Arlington* (1914), 117.

Clarendon, Arlington ten years his junior, the other two pretty well his contemporaries. All four had fought for the King, Jermyn and Arlington somewhat briefly. All had been employed on diplomatic or secret political missions. All of them had been in exile throughout the Interregnum. All had been richly rewarded, many, including Clarendon, thought too richly rewarded, at the Restoration.

The reason for this was that all of them had managed to spend the whole or at least a great part of the exile in close attachment to the King or to his mother or his brother James, Duke of York. And this had meant that Clarendon, as the King's principal adviser from Christmas 1651, had come to know them all too well. He had found them tiresome then. Further experience had intensified the impression. It was the pent-up exasperation of years, further embittered by outrage at their encouragement of the wicked and unjust proceedings of which he was the victim, that drove his pen.

Even so in the first and fullest of these studies, that of George Digby, second Earl of Bristol, his mind rose above his resentment of injuries done him by one who had long been his friend. It is a measure both of Clarendon's wit and of his fundamental good humour that in circumstances of profound unhappiness he could write his comic masterpiece. The character of Digby sparkles as its subject sparkled in life. The charm that bewitched Charles I and his Queen, that conquered, in turn, the Court of France, and of the Spanish Netherlands, that, as he does not conceal, entranced Clarendon himself is rendered in prose as Van Dyck thirty years earlier had rendered it in paint. The artist in Clarendon triumphed over self-love; even more it triumphed over the mental habits of the lawyer and the moralist. Not that these important and deeply characteristic elements do not contribute to the whole. It is simply that when he thought seriously about Digby, about the brilliant and breath-taking adventures of which his life was made up, he found the story and its leading character irresistibly comic. Digby was, in Clarendon's view, directly responsible for much unnecessary personal suffering and for the major political disaster that undid all his own efforts to avert the Civil War, the attempt on the Five Members. This, like the shocking sacrifice of his daughter's happiness,[10] was the stuff of tragedy. But comedy often is. The mode is determined by the angle of vision. Clarendon's presentation of his old friend's character is masterly because without abating a whit of serious criticism it never lets go of the essential absurdity of the man and of the situations he creates for himself. What raises it to the height is that after so subtle and searching an analysis the author declines an explanation. Only Digby himself, he says, can give that. Few writers with Clarendon's fondness for passing judgments could be so self-denying. It is a masterstroke that preserves the integrity of the representation.

The tone of the piece, unlike that of its companions, is fair to the point of magnanimity. Digby had after all attempted to have Clarendon convicted of High Treason and though his ignominious failure had done him more harm than his intended victim, he had behaved ignobly when Clarendon had been hounded out of the country. Alone of these four men he had been a close friend and a close political ally. Like Clarendon he had entered politics in 1640 as an opponent of Strafford, had almost at once won the ear of the House of Commons, had acted, as Clarendon had, in concert with Pym and his friends, indeed had been one of the committee charged with drawing up the charges against Strafford. It was only when the impeachment failed and the contrivers, as Clarendon calls them, went on to move the Act of Attainder, that is to abandon the idea of law and fair play and close in for the kill, that Digby parted company with them. And when he did it he did it in style. He was one of that brave band – Clarendon was not – who faced the rage of former allies, the accusations of treachery, the violence of a mob roused by the placarding of the so-called Straffordians, enemies to their country, who had dared to vote against the Attainder.

[10] See below pp. 92–4.

Clarendon parted company with Pym's friends over the attack on the bishops a few weeks later. But the parallel between their political development was close.

So were their intellectual sympathies. Of all the many improbable but incontestable facts that mark the erratic course of this dazzling young nobleman none is stranger than his authorship of the Letters to his cousin, Sir Kenelm, criticising the grounds of his conversion to the Church of Rome in which he deploys a philosophical skill and a knowledge of the Greek and Latin Fathers that impressed Clarendon, himself the friend of such controversialists as Chillingworth and Falkland.

Digby's father, the first Earl of Bristol, had been an outstandingly able ambassador at Madrid. He was serving there when Buckingham and Charles, then Prince of Wales, arrived to conduct their ludicrous and humiliating courtship of the Infanta. The ambassador incurred the anger and enmity of both by making it plain to them and to the government in London that their activities were mischievous and ill-conceived. He was recalled and disgraced. His brilliant son was offered no place in the royal service. Thus, while Clarendon out of choice spent all the time he could spare in the learned company that gathered at Great Tew, Digby out of necessity had to find employment for his active mind in the library at Sherborne Castle. Unlike Clarendon he was a natural linguist. Brought up in Spain he could pass for a Spaniard. He knew French and Italian by the time he went up to Oxford so that Latin and Greek were easily acquired. His tutor at Magdalen was Peter Heylyn, one of the sharp-shooters of the Laudian party in the Church. Did this turn his mind to theological controversy? It certainly appears an aberration in one so enthusiastically worldly. He seems, indeed, to have thought so himself by Clarendon's account.[11]

But for the moment these two men, so naturally, so strikingly, antithetical, seemed to each other to be in the

[11] See below p. 53.

closest, most intimate sympathy on the great questions of the day. Indeed it was Digby who was largely responsible for introducing Clarendon to the King and engaging him as the secret director of Royalist propaganda.[12] The brilliance claimed for him in the Character seems no exaggeration if compared with another sketch drawn from memory by a contemporary who was never his friend and generally his enemy, Anthony Ashley Cooper, the great Earl of Shaftesbury. Recalling his Dorset neighbours of the days before the Civil War he describes him as 'a very handsome young man of great courage and learning and of a quick wit, [who] began to show himself to the world and gave great expectations of himself, he being justly admired by all, and only gave himself disadvantage with a pedantic stiffness and affectation he had contracted'.[13] It is the one criticism that Clarendon makes of his manner in the House of Commons.

A comparison of the Character written in April 1669 with the shorter description originally written as part of the *Life* very soon afterwards and subsequently incorporated in the *History* (Book IV, 127–8) shows an undiminished admiration for Digby's gifts and acquirements. But it is balanced by sharper, more critical definition. After the extolling of his qualities comes the clinching judgment: 'he was equal to a very good part in the greatest affair, but the unfittest man alive to conduct it, having an ambition and vanity superior to all his other parts, and a confidence peculiar to himself, which sometimes intoxicated and transported and exposed him.' This is Digby seen in the context of history. The exterior effects, not the internal causes, of Digby's being what he was are the writer's concern. In the Character Clarendon is musing on the extraordinary combination of apparently antithetical qualities to be found in the man. The more he reflects the more inexplicable he finds it all. Such

[12] *Life* II, 1 ff. The Earl of Northumberland's brother had brought Clarendon to an interview with the King to receive his thanks for his parliamentary defence of the Church in the summer of 1641 but the real connection was initiated by Digby.

[13] *Memoirs* ed. Christie (1859), 27–8.

graceful agnosticism may be permissible in a private psychological aide-mémoire. It will never do for the historian as
Clarendon understood the functions of the study. Rational
explanation of phenomena and the application of the rules of
morality, divinely inspired and sanctioned, to the conduct of
historical personages are the business of history.

That this more limited approach to the diversity of human
character was enriched by a less inhibited curiosity this
extended study of Digby unforgettably demonstrates. Was it
written as a study in the sense that Rubens or Michelangelo
might make a study of some passage to be incorporated in
some larger composition? If not, what was it? The scale is
much larger than that of the only figure of comparable
importance, Arlington, to be found in this series. Arguably
Sir John Berkeley is projected on the same measurement if
their relative impact on the course of history is taken into
consideration. Berkeley, like Digby, had once been a friend
of Clarendon's. At least Clarendon in many of his letters to
him professes to think so, although it is harder to find
evidence of reciprocal feelings in Berkeley's to him. Perhaps
these pieces were written to help the author clear his mind, to
sum up before coming to a verdict. If so, the intention
remained unfulfilled in every case but Digby's since in the
others the verdict is the first thing we come to.

What is in no doubt is the author's interest in his subject.
He was writing, after all, for himself. Even the *Life*, he
knew, could never be published, even privately, during his
own lifetime. Towards the end of the Digby piece he does
indeed call himself to order: 'I did not intend to have reflected
upon so many particulars, much less to have taken any
survey of the active life of this very considerable person; but
it was hardly possible to give any lively description of his
nature and humour, or any character even of his person and
composition, without representing some instances of particular actions . . .'. The fascination, the puzzle of this subject
carried him away. Or are we to take this interpolation as
literary artifice?

In fact the much briefer description in the *History* tells the reader quite a lot that is not to be found in the Character. We learn, for example, that Digby was by no means on easy terms with Clarendon's closest friend and political ally ' . . . for he was not a man of that exactness as to be in the entire confidence of the lord Falkland, who looked upon his infirmities with more severity than [Colepeper and Clarendon].' Digby's role, both military and political, in the Civil War is minimally treated in the Character. Clarendon's friendship for him is constantly asserted but we are not told that it was to this that Digby owed his appointment as Secretary of State when Falkland was killed in 1643 or that Charles I had pressed Clarendon to take the post himself. On the other hand we are told in categorical terms that Digby was wholly and solely responsible for the attempt on the Five Members. Vindication enough, one would have thought, for the superiority of Falkland's judgment of men.

But where the Character supplies much matter not to be found in the extensive references scattered through the *History* and the *Life* is in the years of exile. It is in these passages that Clarendon comes closest to John Aubrey. He retails the story of Digby's misconceived act of homage to the Duchesse de Châtillon and relaxes into an account of his friend's rituals of courtship that is amusing, detached and uncensorious. Indeed surprisingly for one so strict he appears to approve of this aspect of his life and conduct. 'It is very true,' he writes, 'he was in his constitution, and as much in his nature, very amorous'; and concludes his treatment of the subject with the sentence: 'This wonderful humour continued with him to his age, and I believe will part with him last of all his good qualities . . .'.

The subject is introduced in the first place by Clarendon's asking himself what Digby did with his money. For unlike almost all the other exiles Digby's astonishing power of obtaining offices of profit in whatever country he happened to be meant that he was in a position to be generous. This, conspicuously, he was not. So far from helping a friend he would not even pay his officers. More surprisingly still he spent no money on his person, lacking even the clean linen that the others, however shabby their clothes, still struggled to keep up. Unlike that plutocrat among the impoverished royalists, Jermyn, he spent as little as he could on eating and drinking. But he did share Jermyn's passion for gambling, without, it seems, either the skill or the luck at least to break even. This, and the sacrifices offered to the goddess of the moment, took all he could get.

In spite of reckoning Digby's amours on the credit side Clarendon, surely rightly, ascribes their real power to vanity and self-love. Meanness, that minor vice whose smell carries so much further than most major ones, is yet another manifestation of the egotism that dominated and diminished all Digby's qualities.

The Character tells us virtually nothing about his career after the Restoration. The *Life* gives a clear and notably temperate account of Bristol's[14] attempt to impeach Clarendon in 1663. But Bristol's own conduct in that affair had been so insane that a backcloth of moderation was the most effective means of showing it to the world. To have begun the proceedings by telling the King in front of one of his courtiers that he was so sunk in lechery and idleness that he left the Chancellor to run his kingdom was dumbfounding. At any rate the King was dumbfounded. And when Bristol concluded the audience by threatening him in terms themselves sufficiently treasonable Charles still could not recover from his astonishment enough to call out his Guard and send him to the Tower. This extraordinary scene, recorded by Clarendon from the King's description, is attested by other contemporary authorities such as Pepys's *Diary*. Otherwise the *Life* is on the whole harsher and more summary in its judgments on Bristol than the Character. His extravagance, his graspingness, his ingratitude, his spite, are glanc-

---

[14] Digby succeeded to the Earldom on his father's death in 1653.

ingly noticed. Nowhere are we told anything of Bristol's
new career as a playwright.

The point of no return in the relations between the two
men was Bristol's conversion to Roman Catholicism in 1658.
Clarendon's hostility to that faith was vigorous and lifelong.
As a member of the Great Tew circle it was rational and
informed: if it had not been its strength would deserve to be
called bigoted. Leaving aside its theological basis which he
has in several of his writings argued lucidly enough his
political experience must have weighed heavily against Rome.
In his young manhood a militant Counter-Reformation was
driving all before it in every part of Europe. When he entered
active politics his most relentless enemy was to be found not
among the Great Contrivers but in the heart's affections of
the King he served. Queen Henrietta Maria, with her single-
minded Catholicism, blocked every move he made. After the
defeat of the Royalists in the Civil Wars the keystone of his
policy was to prevent any scheme for restoring Charles II
with the troops and money of one of the great Catholic
powers.

Bristol himself even before his formal adherence to
Catholicism had not accepted this principle. In the Character
and again in the *Life*[15] we are told how easily Mazarin wound
him round his finger in 1646 by promising French support.
No doubt he would have been an even readier advocate of
such a policy in the early 1650s when he rose high in the
Cardinal's favour had Charles II shown any disposition to
listen to him. The change of alliance occasioned by
Cromwell's treaty with the French gave him scope to press
the idea of a Spanish landing in East Anglia from bases in
Flanders in 1657–8. It was his confidence in his standing with
the Spaniards that made it essential, in his eyes, that he
should attend the great Peace Conference at Fuentarabia in
1659. Once the war with the French was out of the way there

---

[15] Subsequently inserted into the *History*, Book X.

would be nothing to stop Spain from restoring his master. In both cases, it appears, the policy of one or other of the two super-powers of the seventeenth century was to be turned from self-interest to knight-errantry by the charm of his personality.

Clarendon saw the matter in a very different light. If France or Spain were to put the King back on his throne, the price would be stiff indeed. Much worse, as a foreign graft on the stock of England it would not take. Worst of all it would identify the Monarchy with Catholicism, even if – and the condition was itself remote – the Church of England were not irretrievably compromised by such a restoration. That Bristol should have counselled such a disastrous course could hardly have surprised or shocked him. His ideas, if acted on, had consistently proved disastrous. It was his conversion to Roman Catholicism that had, at last, to be taken seriously just because it was not serious.

The friendship between the two men had its root in religion and politics. Clarendon might laugh at Bristol's absurdities but he seems, by his own account, to have been unconscionably slow in recognising his frivolity and his complete, childish, self-absorption. The Character reports, with every appearance of verisimilitude, the reactions of Ormonde, of the King and of Clarendon himself to Bristol's announcement of his change of religious allegiance. Ormonde, polite but hardly surprised, said he was sorry to hear it. Charles II laughed heartily, most heartily at Clarendon's expense 'for being so weak a man as to imagine that he [Bristol] could be constant to any profession'. No doubt he was also amused by Bristol's failure to take into account the fact that his religion now disqualified him from his Secretaryship of State and from the Privy Council. He was glad to be rid of him.

Clarendon, it is clear, had at first taken the conversion at face value. He could not understand how so clever and well-read a man could have been brought to alter his convictions by so buffle-headed a cleric as the English Provincial of the

Jesuits, Father Courteney. It was only the raised eyebrows of Ormonde and the open derision of the King that sowed a doubt. Bristol was not serious about serious things. He had become a Papist not because his convictions had changed but because his perceptions of his own self-interest had. He was looking for high preferment under the Spanish Crown, not for the restoration of the English one. He belonged, after all, to the same inferior category as the other three sitters in this small gallery, Berkeley, Arlington and Jermyn. It was scarcely credible, that a man of such brilliant gifts, such reckless courage, such panache, could be content to be so ordinary.

Yet the moral judgment to which Clarendon felt himself compelled did not, as in so many other instances in the *History* and the *Life*, close the matter with a lapidary phrase. It left him with a question. The parts were so much greater than the whole that there must be either a mistake in the arithmetic or a puzzle, a mystery, perhaps caused by some unresolved element in the character. When Charles II remarked, as reported by Pepys, that Bristol could make a fortune in any country in three years and would lose it in three months he epitomised his career. But what Clarendon wanted was to explain it. His triumph is to accept his inability to do so.

For his part Bristol never accepted the disadvantageous consequences of his own actions. If things went wrong someone else was to blame. His exclusion from the Council was thus not the direct, indeed inevitable, result of his change of religion but could only be attributed to the malice and jealousy of Clarendon. From Fuentarabia he therefore made his way to Madrid, sure of a welcome as his father's son and already distinguished by the favours shown him in the Spanish Netherlands. He was indeed graciously received. Although not offered the high office or great command for which he had hoped he was given a good sum of money with which to continue his travels. He had originally projected a visit to Rome but the sudden change of wind in England that carried the Royalists home caught him unawares. He returned by way of Paris, pausing to make his peace with Mazarin who had refused him a pass to the conference at Fuentarabia and, when he had made his way there incognito, would not grant him an audience. It was late June or early July 1660 by the time he was back in London.

As in Madrid he was courteously received and presented with an even larger sum of money, £10,000. But the great offices of State, even the Council Chamber, were still closed to him. The Catholicism which had seemed such a prudent re-insurance against the continued misfortunes of the Stuarts had left him between two stools. The Spaniards preferred not to employ him: and in the climate of 1660 it was not possible that Charles should. Once again Clarendon was the focus of Bristol's resentment. Nothing but his displacement would open the way to reward commensurate to his own merit. Clarendon had accepted the continuation of the Anglo-French alliance initiated by Cromwell and had underwritten the negotiations for a Portuguese marriage inspired by the Earl of Manchester and supported by Manchester's cousin, the newly created Earl of Sandwich. This was looked on with horror in Madrid since in Spanish eyes Portugal was simply a province in revolt, not a separate kingdom, and the house of Braganza was ducal not royal. Once its status had been enhanced by intermarriage with the Crown of England it would be very much harder to induce anyone else, particularly the Portuguese, to take this view.

Bristol therefore saw an opening for his own special relationship with the Spanish government. If he could overturn the Anglo-Portuguese alliance what might he not hope for? He might even displace Clarendon himself. And the ground on which the contest was to be determined was very much his own. He had all the languages and Clarendon had none. He had been bred in one of the best embassies in Europe. He had all the arts of the courtier. And the King would certainly trust his judgment of feminine allure above that of his Lord Chancellor.

From the account Clarendon gives in his autobiography[16] this wild venture came alarmingly near to success. The negotiations with Portugal had been virtually completed by the time Bristol arrived, a fact of which both King and Chancellor kept him in ignorance. But Bristol, supported by a somewhat aggressive Spanish ambassador, played the gynaecological card for all it was worth. The ambassador had already disparaged Catherine of Braganza's looks and personal attractions in language so offensive as to sting Charles II's pride. Bristol assured the King with a wealth of detail that her sexual underdevelopment rendered her incapable of bearing children. The inference that Clarendon himself must have known this and had pressed the marriage to secure the succession of his own grandchildren could safely be left to an intelligence so quick and so cynical as the King's. On the positive side the Spaniards offered to match the dowry agreed with the Portuguese and the subsidy secretly promised by the French, who wanted nothing more than that Spain should continue to be embroiled in a war with Portugal and, if possible, England as well. Although no Infanta was available at Madrid there were two Princesses in the Spanish dominions in Italy whose personal charms Bristol vouched for in terms that Clarendon considered hardly decent. Who can doubt that he found the King an attentive listener? The diplomatic machinery that had been humming busily away faltered and came to a standstill. Clarendon, deeply disturbed, warned the King that his honour was at stake. If he wanted to extricate himself from the marriage, diplomatic obstacles could easily be contrived to cover his retreat. But he must be off with the old love before he was on with the new.

This interview took place shortly after an exultant Bristol, privately commissioned by the King to survey the Italian ladies so invitingly described, had set off for the continent. On the eve of his departure he had disclosed to an astonished Clarendon the nature of his mission and had charged his old

[16] Cont., 164ff.

friend not to do anything that might frustrate it. The King, as might be expected, had not taken him into his confidence as to how far things had gone with the Portuguese. Clarendon considered himself bound by his Privy Counsellor's oath not to disclose it. He therefore, by his own account relying on Bristol's 'incredible power to make himself believe anything he had a mind should be true', contented himself with vague good wishes for the journey.

Under pressure from Clarendon and his senior colleagues, Southampton and Ormonde, the King agreed to send Bristol a message of recall. This, Clarendon tells us, probably reached him before he had crossed into Italy though Bristol afterwards denied this. His scheme might still have come off – the King liked discomfiting his ministers – had the Spanish ambassador not ruined everything by overplaying his hand. Charles II was morbidly sensitive to any suggestion that he was managed by his servants. But to be threatened and dictated to by a foreign monarch was not to be endured. The Portugal Treaty was signed and sealed, the new Parliament greeted with the news of the King's forthcoming marriage, while Bristol was still in Italy. His fury, and its target, can easily be imagined. Once again it was Clarendon, that false friend, who had undone him, indeed deliberately deceived him. The violence of his reaction erupted in the attempted impeachment of 1663. The effect was, as we have seen, the opposite of that intended. Only after Clarendon's fall in 1667 did Bristol dare to show his face in the House of Lords.

Thereafter his bitterness against his old friend yielded some profit. In the middle of November, a fortnight before the King ordered Clarendon into exile, Pepys reported he was once again in the King's good graces. In the following April he was granted a patent to superintend banks and Monts de Piété in London, Westminster and other cities with power to appoint deputies. Presumably it was not his knowledge of finance which recommended him for this appointment. His own, in spite of this latest favour, remained in perpetual disorder. On 22 January 1669 he submitted a vast petition detailing the payments allegedly due to him to Arlington, then Secretary of State, whose first employer he had been when himself Secretary of State at Oxford in 1643. Arlington annotated it and five months later supported its claims in a report signed by himself and his co-Secretary of State, Sir John Trevor. Lord Keeper Bridgeman approved their liberal assessment and, at length, on 7 June 1670 a warrant was issued for a payment that included a pension of £2000 a year and £10,000 in cash. On the strength of this Bristol bought on 4 September the governorship of Deal Castle for his younger son. Within a week he was reported to be keeping a great house there to celebrate the inauguration of the new governor. To the last his optimism seems to have been preserved from any taint of experience. Only a month later he was begging Arlington's help. The revenues assigned him had not been paid. He was, as always, deep in debt.[17]

To the last he continued to live with something of the magnificence proper to his rank. The Sherborne estate had long gone to settle his debts and the fines imposed by the Parliament but his wife, who had remained in England during the Interregnum, had bought it back with her jointure and settled it on their eldest son at the time of his marriage. After the Restoration he bought the splendid house at Wimbledon that Lambert, himself a notable gardener, had lived in during Cromwell's time. It had previously belonged to Henrietta Maria and reverted to her in 1660. She sold it to him in 1661 and early the next year Bristol took John Evelyn out to advise him on laying out the garden in the new style. 'It is a delicious place for Prospect, & the thicketts, but the soile cold and weeping clay.'[18] He also inherited a mansion in Great Queen Street from his father, which was let to the Council for Foreign Plantations in 1670.[19] As late as 1674 he bought the great house in Chelsea which had belonged to Sir

---

[17] See *Cal. S.P. Dom.* under the dates cited.

[18] *Diary* iii, 316.

[19] *ibid.* 577–8.

Thomas More. It was here that he died in 1677, three years after Clarendon.

His last conspicuous appearance in politics recaptured the unexpectedness of his early Parliamentary career. In the debate on the Test Act in 1673 he spoke, though an avowed Roman Catholic, in favour of the measure. A Protestant country, he argued, had a perfect right to defend its political and ecclesiastical institutions. 'I am a Catholic of the Church of Rome, not of the Court of Rome.' The moderation of these sentiments would perhaps have carried more conviction if the record of the speaker had been less violent and erratic. And in any case how profound was his attachment to the Church of Rome? In January 1664 while still a fugitive from arrest he had startled the congregation at Wimbledon parish church by a public abjuration of Roman Catholicism after which he had received the sacrament. Soon afterwards this recantation was itself recanted.[20] Did Clarendon, one wonders, hear of the Test Act speech in his exile at Moulins? Probably. It certainly supports his view of his old friend and bitter enemy.

Sir John Berkeley, first Lord Berkeley of Stratton, was one of the very few friends whom Clarendon addressed, and referred to, not only by his Christian name but by the familiar form 'Jack'. Over the centuries no convention seems to have been more strict, less open to local or temporary difference of usage, than that governing the use of Christian names in polite society. Even by late Victorian times it was rare outside the family or the household to use Christian names. Trollope's faithfulness to nature is proverbial. In *The Warden* (1855) Mrs Grantly addresses her husband as 'Archdeacon' even in the privacy of their bedroom. Thirty years later Cardinal Newman began a letter of intimate affection to a dying man, 'My very dear Pattison'.

---

[20] Pepys's *Diary*, v, 58–9 and note.

Clarendon was formal in his habit of address. Letters to his closest friends and colleagues, Ormonde and Nicholas for instance, are often emotional, even passionate; but however high his feelings are running, title or office – 'Oh Mr. Secretary!' – are soberly respected. Nicknames, particularly those in effect formalised by regular use, are permissible when writing to a young friend of the family; Secretary Nicholas's son John is generally addressed as 'My good Tutour'. His own wife is 'My deare little rogue'. Falkland and he were 'Deare Sweetheart' to each other: the jocularity, perhaps, of entire want of reserve. Very rarely Clarendon uses such familiarity with people whom he did not in fact like, as when he addresses Daniel O'Neile as 'Infallible, subtle'.[21]

Why was Berkeley so excepted? Perhaps because he alone of the Royalist exiles with whom Clarendon corresponded had been a friend from the days of their young manhood in London. When the breach between them came in 1653 Clarendon told Lady Morton that he had been Berkeley's 'fast and unshaken friend, and the best he ever had, or will have, for the space of twenty years'.[22] 1633, it will be remembered, is the date of the Jermyn-Villiers scandal that first brought the young Mr Hyde into the circle of the court. Berkeley was already established there.

If Bristol's career astonishes by the disproportion between richness of talent and poverty of achievement, Berkeley's is no less puzzling for the opposite reason. Why was he chosen to go as ambassador to Christina of Sweden in 1636 in the hopes of inducing her to champion the cause of the Elector Palatine? In the *D.N.B.* his kinship to Sir Thomas Roe, the outstanding English diplomat of his age, has been suggested. This relationship is however too faint to be discernible. The idea of it probably arose from confusing Sir John with his very remote cousin Sir Maurice Berkeley, who was indeed

[21] Clar. MS 46 f.361, 31 Oct. 1653.

[22] *ibid.* 45 f.111.

Sir Thomas Roe's favourite nephew.* The court and diplomatic connections of his mother's family, the Killigrews,
seem to offer a likelier explanation.

For his failure in what was anyhow likely to fail he was
knighted. Like another of his useful relations, Henry Jermyn,
he seems to have stood well with the Queen, a connection
that he was to exploit during the years of exile. But in 1637
he began, in the army that the King was raising to coerce the
Scots, the military career in which he was to do rather better
than Clarendon admits in the Character (the *History* is less
grudging) if not so well as he was himself too ready to claim.
Neither of these activities would have brought him into the
world of a rising barrister with literary and intellectual tastes.
The only circumstance of life that might have formed a bond
was that of geography. Berkeley's father's estate was at
Bruton, not far from the Hyde clan's west Wiltshire holdings.
In the Short Parliament of 1640 Berkeley and Hyde were
both returned for Wiltshire constituencies. Not that Berkeley
was a House of Commons man, as Hyde was. He was a
courtier through and through, though never satisfied with
what others thought the substantial rewards of his profession.

The Character suggests that as a young man he was
attractive and well-liked: that he was even modest and in-
dustrious, travelling to France and Spain to learn languages
and taking service in Germany, as so many young gentlemen
did, to learn the business of an officer. It was his early
preferment and his knighthood that spoiled him: and the
process was irreversibly carried forward by his being made
Governor of Exeter in 1643. In this piece justice is perhaps
stinted to the enterprise and courage that he showed early in
the Civil War when he and Hopton under the nominal
command of the eminently unmilitary Marquis of Hertford
occupied Sherborne Castle, the seat of the Digbys, in the face
of a Parliamentary force that outnumbered them by three to
one, kept them out of the town, beat up their quarters and

---

* I am indebted to Roe's biographer, Mr. Michael Strachan, for this information.

finally drove them off with their tails between their legs. The psychological effect of such an action was disproportionate. It was generally assumed that the King, having lost London and every major port, his navy and his arsenals, before the war had even begun was bound to sue for peace. And the victory early in 1643 from which Berkeley, perhaps presumptuously, was later to take his title was an even more valuable performance, again won against heavy odds. Hopton and Sir Bevil Grenville, to whom Berkeley was second-in-command, were its true architects. But Berkeley's part in the action was not inconsiderable.[23]

The Governorship of Exeter, in which Clarendon considered Berkeley showed lack of military initiative, brought a stroke of luck that consolidated his already promising career as a courtier. It was to Exeter that the Queen, expecting a child and anxious to secure a safe retreat to France, came in the spring of 1644. She was attended by Lady Dalkeith, the sister of the maid of honour whom Jermyn had seduced, and, from that time, a close friend of Clarendon. Here the Queen's last child and youngest daughter Henriette was born. But the mother, in poor health and deeply agitated by the threatening prospect of Royalist defeat, left the baby in the care of Lady Dalkeith and took ship for France. In all this Berkeley was useful to her. When she had gone he advanced money of his own for the support of the little Princess and her lady in waiting.[24] After the war was over he and Lady Dalkeith were both to join Henrietta Maria in Paris.

In the closing stages of the war he and Hyde renewed their friendship. These were the anxious days when Hyde, charged by Charles I with the safety of the Prince of Wales, found himself dependent for the security of the Prince and for intelligence of enemy movements and Royalist dispositions on commanders such as Goring and Sir Richard Grenville who could not be relied on in anything except to quarrel with

[23] On these actions see Peter Young and Richard Holmes, *The English Civil War* (1974).

[24] *Cal. Clar. S.P.* ii, 21, 81, 104.

each other as to precedence and subordination. In this scene of confusion and collapse Berkeley stood for honesty and trust, at any rate by the account given in the *History*.[25] The excellent terms which he eventually obtained for the surrender of the place in April 1646, when Hyde and the Prince had left England, are remarked by S. R. Gardiner.[26] They included the liberty of the little Princess and her lady. Fuller, who was then in Exeter as Berkeley's chaplain, comments in his *Worthies* that no better terms were obtained anywhere at the end of the war and none were so well kept.[27]

Clarendon in the Character here printed disparages Berkeley's achievement, implying that it was discreditable to surrender so strong and well provisioned a place and that the best terms were always given to those who had held out to the last biscuit. Partly this judgment may be attributed to the low opinion he had come to hold of him by the time he was writing. But there was a particular cause rankling in his mind. Berkeley himself had concluded from the liberality of the terms that he was in some special sense *persona grata* with the Parliamentary Army, particularly with Fairfax and Cromwell. It was this confidence in his standing with them that prevailed with the Queen to send him over from Paris to act as intermediary in the negotiations between the King and the Army officers when Charles was their prisoner in 1647.

Clarendon, writing in 1669, puts all this down to Berkeley's vanity. There is no reason, he suggests, to believe that Cromwell and Ireton thought anything of him. They welcomed him because they recognised how easy it would be to manipulate a man of such mediocre understanding. On the assumption, which is cardinal to the whole thesis of the *History*, that Cromwell was an arch-dissembler who from the first had been scheming to obtain dictatorial powers this makes sense. But what if he was not? What if he really

[25] See Bk ix, especially the deleted passage at ix, 82.

[26] *History of the Great Civil War* (1889) ii, 465.

[27] *op. cit.* Devonshire, 273.

have rubbed his eyes or snorted with derision at Gardiner's portrayal of his modest sense of own insufficiency,[30] later identified as 'characteristic'.[31] A host of contemporary witnesses, Pepys among them, would support Clarendon's insistence that his vanity was prodigious.

The part played by Berkeley in the conduct of these negotiations was even on his own evidence[32] superficial. He was not in the King's confidence and had therefore to be supported by another courtier, Ashburnham, who was. Both men, as their Memoirs testify, were jealous of each other. Neither emerges from their respective essays in self-justification as at all impressive. Both, together with Ashburnham's fellow gentleman of the King's bedchamber, Colonel Legge, were now to share the responsibility for the mishandling of Charles's flight from Hampton Court. There seems little doubt that the prime mover in the business was Cromwell.[33] The King's brusque rejection of the Heads of Proposals, with which he and Ireton had hoped to dish the Presbyterian party and check the advance of radicalism in the army, had left him dangerously exposed to an attack on two fronts. The King was no longer a trump card but a threat. To play on his fear of assassination was an easy method of inducing him to dispose of himself. Ashburnham, Berkeley and Legge seemed not to have noticed how few difficulties presented themselves to the escape of so important a figure. None of them, it must be admitted, was among the cleverest of the King's servants.

Berkeley, by his own account, at least insisted on making sure of 'three or four ships in several ports, to be ready in all events'. This was at a Sunday lunch of the three conspirators at Thames Ditton immediately before the plan was put into

[30] *ibid.* iii, 146.

[31] *ibid.* 171–2.

[32] Both Berkeley and Ashburnham wrote their accounts of these events before 1672 since Clarendon explicitly states that he had read them. Berkeley's Memoirs were first printed in 1699. As he is styled 'Sir John' they must antedate his elevation to the peerage in 1658.

[33] See Christopher Hill, *God's Englishman* (1970), 96–8.

execution. The vagueness of the conception is breath-taking. Where *was* the King making for? France? The Channel Islands? Ireland? Scotland? The choice of an objective should surely have preceded the staff work. But that some ship would have to be at instant notice for sea might be taken as implicit in any plan of escape. Berkeley records that the others 'seemed to concur; but nothing was ever done in it: which to this day amazes me'.

His amazement has been generally shared by every hearer of the story that ended in Carisbrooke Castle. Clarendon, who knew all the participants, had access to all the contemporary evidence, read all the statements of Berkeley and Ashburnham and subsequently interrogated them 'at large', gives by far the best account in the tenth book of the *History*. Ugly insinuations were made by contemporaries against both Ashburnham and Berkeley but Clarendon refuses to subscribe to them. The key to his explanation of the affair, in so far as it is explicable, is to be found in the parenthesis 'nor do I in truth think that the King himself, when he took horse, resolved whither to go'. The whole thing was a game of blind man's buff. What is noticeable in both the *History* and the present work is that Berkeley is exonerated from any responsibility whatever. It was only his own absurd vanity that had ever misled anyone into thinking that he was more than a glorified groom, told to have the horses saddled at such and such a time and place. In the *History* Clarendon very fairly gives him credit for offering to remain a hostage at Carisbrooke, which Ashburnham had declined to do. The King's whereabouts were still unknown to the Parliamentary governor and there would have been the chance of a get-away. Clarendon's suggestion that Berkeley comes out of the business better than Ashburnham receives interesting negative confirmation from that fairest, least malicious, of historical witnesses, Sir Philip Warwick:

'I never had occasion but once at the Isle of Wight to speak with the King about this affair; and it was by accident, or the King's letting himselfe into that discourse: and he did but touch upon it, nor durst I seem to be more inquisitive. But when I mentioned that the world had an ill opinion of my friend Mr. Ashburnham's guiding him thither, I remember, he freely replied, *I do no way believe, he was unfaithful to me; but I think he wanted courage at that time*; (which I interpreted, His Majestie meant his not staying with the Governour) *whom I never knew wanted it before.*'[34]

The King was conducted to Carisbrooke on 14 November. Still confident of his power to play off his opponents against each other he sent Berkeley to the Army Headquarters at Windsor to propose a personal treaty that would outflank Parliament. The offer was flatly rejected. While at Windsor Berkeley was informed by a direct message from Cromwell that he dare not compromise himself by further negotiation with the King towards whom he expressed a slightly equivocal goodwill. This was reinforced by a secret nocturnal visitor, unnamed by Berkeley, who warned him that Cromwell and Ireton had thrown the King over. This was at the end of November. A month later Berkeley, dismissed along with Ashburnham and Legge from attendance at Carisbrooke by order of the governor, crossed over to the mainland. According to his own account three weeks later he went back to France. In fact his movements seem not to have been quite so rapid. On 17 January Sir Edward Nicholas at Caen told Hyde's secretary in Jersey that both Berkeley and Ashburnham were still seeking a passage across the Channel.[35] Three days later the Earl of Manchester at Derby House informed Colonel Hammond that the pair were at Netley Abbey.[36] There seems no reason to doubt Berkeley's own statement that, beginning to despair, he moved that one of them should be sent as messenger to the Queen and that the other two agreed and chose him.

From Paris the Queen sent him early in May to The Hague as acting governor to the young Duke of York who had

[34] *Memoires* (1701), 306.
[35] *Cal. Clar. S.P.* i, 408.
[36] *C.S.P. Dom.* 20 Jan 48.

broken his parole and escaped from St James's Palace. The sophistical arguments by which he had been induced to compromise his honour and the woman's clothes in which he had travelled had both been provided by a picturesque scoundrel called Colonel Bampfield whom Henrietta Maria in a rare flash of judgment seems to have recognised as untrustworthy. She therefore despatched Berkeley to lend some respectability and, it was hoped, discretion to the Duke's affairs. His proper governor Lord Byron was deeply involved in the preparations for the second Civil War that was on the point of breaking out. Having commanded in the North-West he was charged with assisting the Scots invasion under Hamilton and, after that had been defeated, joined Ormonde in Ireland. It was not until early in the following year that he presented himself on the continent ready to resume his duties.

Meanwhile Berkeley was enjoying the importance and the perquisites of the position. One of his recommendations for it in the Queen's eyes was that Bampfield had served under him in the early days of the Civil War. But Clarendon in the *History*, written two or three years after the Character, suggests that their comradeship in arms had not been a happy one: ' . . . which Bampfield looked upon as a degradation, and bringing the man he hated of all men living to have the command over him'.[37] Bampfield had been rewarded by being made groom of the Duke's bedchamber. Resentful of losing the standing of principal adviser he seized on the opportunity offered by the revolt of the Parliamentary Fleet in the Downs and its arrival in the harbour of Helvoetsluys at the end of May. Here was a chance to turn the tables on his old commanding officer, who had, according to Clarendon, already succeeded in making himself unpopular with the Duke and his domestic circle. Bampfield went aboard the English ships, and having, as his career abundantly attests, the gift of the gab induced the sailors and their officers to

[37] *Hist.* XI, 21.

declare that the Duke, then a boy of fourteen, should be their Admiral. James accepted with alacrity and lost no time in appointing his subordinate flag-officers. Naturally these proceedings did not commend themselves to the Prince of Wales when, a few days later, he arrived hotfoot from Paris. There was a row between the brothers and Bampfield's intrigues in the matter led to his dismissal by the Prince from his attendance on the Duke. The clinching point was a message from the captive King himself, who had previously employed Bampfield as a secret agent, strictly forbidding him access to his son. Bampfield returned to England and a successful career as a double-agent working for Thurloe. He experienced one or two nasty moments at the Restoration but like so many thorough-going rascals survived into a ripe old age.

Even James, Duke of York, was brought by his father's admonition to recognise that Bampfield was not an appropriate companion. But it did not endear Sir John Berkeley to him. He liked to choose his own servants and he at first resented Berkeley's being imposed on him by his mother as he was later to resent Henry Bennet's being imposed on him by his brother. None the less Berkeley held on. Byron did not return to claim his place until the spring of 1649.[38] Bennet, whose appointment as Secretary was to lead to a historical chain-reaction counting among its effects the elevation of Berkeley to the peerage, was already attached to the Duke's household. Clarendon in the Character (below p. 118) asserts that it was through his connexions with the Queen's court at Paris that he obtained the appointment. There exists in the Clarendon State Papers a list, drawn up in Berkeley's hand and dated 12 November 1648, of servants to attend the Duke of York at sea.[39] Its amplitude seems somewhat fanciful. There is a barber, a yeoman of the robes, a stitcher to the robes and several flunkeys. It is headed by Sir John Berkeley

[38] D.N.B. authorities cited.

[39] Cal. Clar. S.P. i, 445.

with three servants and Mr. Bennet with one. Five days later
the Prince of Wales cancelled these arrangements by resolving
not to venture his brother's person at sea and ordering him to
the Brill.[40] Soon afterwards the Revolted Fleet sailed for
Ireland under the more realistic command of Prince Rupert.

Until Byron arrived Berkeley was in charge of a disgruntled
and quarrelsome adolescent. Bennet, by Clarendon's account
no less vain and ambitious than Berkeley, was exasperated at
finding himself junior to a man of such second-rate abilities.
As his future with the Duke was blocked he set out to make
ground with the young Charles II by acting as a spy on his
brother. Had the young King been less easy-going 'he had
then kindled a jealousy between the two brothers and indeed
did go so far towards it that the Duke put him out of his
service'.[41] Berkeley is not named but is easily identifiable in
the passage as the object of Bennet's jealousy.

On Byron's reappearance it was Berkeley's turn to sulk.
He applied for, and obtained, the King's agreement to his
going as ambassador to Turkey.[42] Unfortunately there was
the little matter of the money – £1,000 – which the merchants
declined to advance. No more was heard of this project.
Clarendon's cousin who subsequently undertook this mission
was kidnapped by his Commonwealth rival and executed for
High Treason so perhaps Berkeley's usual luck had held. He
was certainly fortunate in letting his offended pride keep him
behind in Paris when his young master went off on his hare-
brained expedition to Brussels to seek the alliance of the
exiled Duke of Lorraine. This was to risk the capricious
goodwill of France, such as it was, for no compensating
advantage. Henrietta Maria was horrified. She insisted that
Byron and Bennet should accompany the Duke even though
they were unlikely to be consulted. She even pressed
Clarendon, hardly her favourite minister, to seek out her

[40] *ibid.* 446.

[41] Below p.130.

[42] *Clar. S.P.* ii, 531. Berkeley to Hyde 22 March 1650.

rebellious son on his return to Flanders from his embassy in Madrid and bring him back into the fold. This he succeeded in, so that at the end of 1651 after the King's escape from England the Royal family were reunited in Paris.

It was at this point that Berkeley had another stroke of luck. Lord Byron died. Without waiting to see whether or not he was to be appointed governor in his place Berkeley infuriated Clarendon by styling himself *Intendant des affaires de son altesse royale*.[43] This might annoy Clarendon but it was highly acceptable to the young Duke as confirming his own opinion that he no longer needed a governor. Berkeley had at last begun to work himself into his good graces by championing the Duke's ambition of embarking on a career in the French army under Turenne. Both the King and the Queen had reservations as to hazarding the life of the heir presumptive when the future of the Crown itself was uncertain enough.[44] It was, by his own account, Clarendon who eventually devised a formula that satisfied all parties, namely that while it would not have been right for the King to propose or even to approve such a course it would not be right for him to obstruct it.[45]

Thus Clarendon was, if we accept his version of events, instrumental in promoting the cause on which Berkeley's subsequent prosperity was founded. But before this took place Berkeley had in set form declared an end to their friendship. The account Clarendon gives in the *History* sounds true as far as it goes. But it omits, properly in such a work, personal and private reasons. Their correspondence preserved in the Clarendon MSS in the Bodleian Library, much of it printed or calendared, shows that for the past five or six years their politics had diverged and that Berkeley, perhaps with some justice, resented the superior tone of pity and reproof with which his old friend addressed him. There was also the

---

[43] *Hist.* XIII, 148.

[44] *ibid.* 122.

[45] *ibid.* 128.

far more delicate question of Berkeley's courtship of the widowed Countess of Morton (as Lady Dalkeith had become on the death of her father-in-law). It seems clear, and Berkeley evidently believed, that Clarendon, who was himself deeply attached to the lady, had advised against his suit.[46]

But none of this gives any reason for doubting the general truth of the story told in the *History*.[47] When Charles II returned to Paris at the end of 1651 and sent for Clarendon he had no other Privy Counsellors to serve him. Clearly the Council must be enlarged, and equally clearly respect must be paid to the position of Henrietta Maria as the aunt of the sovereign whose hospitality was extended to the exiled court. Jermyn therefore was admitted, though neither the King nor Clarendon had any opinion of him. Lord Wilmot, Charles's boon companion who had shared his adventures on the run after the defeat at Worcester, could hardly be refused. Ormonde who had been Lord Lieutenant of Ireland was an obvious and valuable reinforcement. So too, in his own estimation, would have been Sir John Berkeley. But though he was a great favourite with the Queen Charles II disliked him and resented his pretensions. These he most unwisely heightened to include the Mastership of the Wards, a post traditionally regarded as carrying an *ex officio* right to a place in the Council. That the claim was absurd was easily shown. Berkeley based it on an alleged promise of Charles I to the Queen: the Parliament however had captured, and published, the letter of which the relevant passage ran, 'As for Jack Barclay I do not remember that I gave thee any hope of making him Master of the Wards. For Cottington had it long ago before thou went hence.' That it was in the highest degree inexpedient to fill the office, now void by Cottington's death, was equally obvious. As Clarendon pointed out to his master he could hardly take a step which would instantly antagonise more of the nobility and gentry than that of

[46] On this see my *Clarendon and his friends.*

[47] *op. cit.* XIII, 122–7.

showing, or even suggesting, that he was going to reconstitute the most hated of the feudal rights that even his father had consented to part with, that of wardship and livery. Charles took the point but, to avoid irritating his mother and brother by directly refusing their protégé, temporised. He could do nothing for the moment but perhaps the matter might be looked at again. Pushing his luck Berkeley pressed him for a straight answer yes or no and got the second.

'All this,' wrote Clarendon, 'he imputed to the Chancellor' on the grounds that the reasons the King had given for refusing his request were exactly those his old friend had previously advanced in attempting to dissuade him from urging his claims. The scene came back to him as he recorded it. He remembered Berkeley's very calm though very confused manner as they walked together in the long gallery at the Louvre – a detail that he subsequently struck out of the manuscript. Berkeley gave him notice that the friendship between them was ended and 'that they might live towards each other with that civility only that strangers use to do. . . . And so they parted, without ever after having conversation with each other whilst they remained in France'.

Those years were, for Clarendon, the unhappiest and most humiliating of his life. His relations with the Queen became more and more strained. The King soon slipped into the indolence and undesirable company against which his great minister was to remonstrate ineffectively for the next fifteen years. To poverty, to a growing sense of frustration, was added the grief of separation from his wife and children. Berkeley on the other hand was riding high. The Duke of York's military apprenticeship to Turenne was a resounding success. 'The Knight' as Clarendon often calls him in his private correspondence was not diffident in taking credit for this happy issue. And the Duke's affection and loyalty, slowly won, were not shallow. As his star rose, a Lieutenant-General in the French army in his early twenties, his brother's declined. Mazarin was moving towards his treaty of alliance with Cromwell and money spent on relieving the necessities

of Charles II was money thrown away. The courtiers who
were later to cluster round the King, Charles Berkeley, Bab
May and the rest, elbowed their way towards the abundance
of the Duke.[48] When the Treaty was signed in 1654 and the
King was ordered to leave France he set out from Paris on
horseback with his possessions in a box strapped on the
crupper.

Charles II would not have been human if he had not felt
some jealousy at his brother's happier circumstances. No
doubt it gave him some pleasure to make a treaty in his turn
with the Spaniards which required the Duke of York to lay
down his commission in the French army and to enter the
service of Spain. Both James and Digby, now Earl of Bristol,
had been retained as officers of the French army seconded to
service in Italy in order to satisfy the conditions of the Anglo-
French treaty. But Cromwell was anxious to root out any
element of Stuart dynastic pretension in the eyes of his ally.
This was the period at which he was certainly considering the
pros and cons of taking the Crown himself. It was thus some
two years after Charles II's departure that James, attended by
Sir John Berkeley, arrived in the Spanish Netherlands. His
dismissal from the French service had been as courteous, as
regretful, as Mazarin knew how to make it. Turenne and the
Duke parted from each other with the sincerest expressions
of friendship and esteem. James indeed had made it a condition
of his exchange of employment that he should not be required
to confront his old commander in battle.

He was thus not disposed to submit to off-hand treatment
from his brother, who had in any case irritated him by
appointing Bennet, whom James loathed, as his secretary and
principal adviser on his leaving Paris in 1654. The antagonism
between Berkeley and Bennet had, as Clarendon earlier
recorded, come close to making bad blood between the King
and the Duke. This time it succeeded. Bennet persuaded the
King that Berkeley was making mischief and the King forbade

[48] *Cal. Clar. S.P.* ii, 304.

him the court. The Duke, outraged, deployed his usual tactics of leaving the country, in this case crossing the Dutch frontier to stay with his sister, the Princess of Orange.

An open split in the Royal family was one of Cromwell's principal objectives at this time. That Berkeley was his instrument is clear from the following paragraphs of a letter he wrote to Mazarin at this time. Was he, consciously or deludedly, his agent?

'And now I shall come to return to your Eminency thanks for your judicious choice of that person to whom you have intrusted our weightiest affair, an affair wherein your Eminency is concerned, though not in equal degree and measure with myself. I must confess that I have had some doubts of its success, till providence cleared them to me by the effects, I was not truly, and to speak ingenuously, without doubting; I did fear that Berkley would not have been able to go through and carry on that work, that either the Duke had cooled in his suit, or condescended to his Brother; I doubted also that those instructions which I had sent over with 290 were not clear enough as to expressions, some affairs here denying me leisure at that time to be so particular as to some circumstances I would. If I am not mistaken in his character, as I received it from your Eminency, that fire which is kindled between them now will not ask bellows to blow it or keep it burning. But what I think further necessary in this matter I will send your Eminency by Lockhart.*

And now I shall boast to your Eminency my security, upon a well-builded confidence in the Lord, for I distrust not but if this breach be widened a little more, and this difference fomented with some caution in respect of the person to be added to it, I distrust not but that Party, which is already forsaken of God (as to outward dispensations of mercy) and noysome to his Countrymen, will

* Sir William Lockhart, Cromwell's ambassador in Paris.

grow lower in the opinions of all the world. If I have troubled your Eminency too long in this, you may repute it to the resentment of joy I have for the issue of that affair.'[49]

The questions raised by this letter are so tantalising that one can only wonder at the silence with which historians, not least Clarendon, have passed it by. Whatever construction may be put on it must be deeply damaging to Berkeley. Why did Clarendon not use it? He was writing of course without access to his own documentary collections but he would hardly have forgotten a letter from Oliver to Mazarin that contained such dynamite. Did Henry only obtain it at a later date so that his father never saw it? The alternative explanation is that Clarendon was still hoping that one day Charles II would relent and allow him to return from exile. It was well to be careful what one put on paper. There was not only Berkeley's reputation to be considered. The story, if it ever came out, might reflect on the Duke of York.

None of these considerations applies to Berkeley's nineteenth-century champion, S. R. Gardiner. Rushing to that magisterial succession of volumes one is tantalised again. Death claimed the great man just as he was coming to this point. But his faithful disciple Sir Charles Firth took up the pen where Gardiner laid it down. He certainly knew the letter (as surely Gardiner must have) since he actually prints part of it which replies to Mazarin's request for increased toleration for Roman Catholics.[50] But he says nothing of the Protector's plan for sowing discord between the Stuart brothers, assisted, in descending order, by the Almighty, the Cardinal and Sir John Berkeley.

Charles II and Clarendon were so alert to the threat that they set off on a journey of reconciliation, in the course of

---

[49] *Clar. S.P.* iii, 319. Copy in the hand of Henry Hyde from a document originally supplied by one of Cromwell's chaplains. There is no doubt of the authenticity as it is to be found in *Thurloe S.P.* v, 735 and the French archives.

[50] C. H. Firth *The Last Years of the Protectorate* i, 78.

which the King was nearly a victim of a musketry salute. The terms of the settlement represented a victory for the Duke. The hated Bennet was taken out of his entourage and sent as ambassador to Madrid. Sir John Berkeley was not only admitted to the Court but was promised a peerage as Lord Berkeley of Stratton, much to Clarendon's disapproval, 'he having no pretence of any one acre of land in the world, nor being worth the cloaths he wore'.[51] Thus the two men whose selfish irresponsibility had prejudiced the whole Royalist cause at a moment of dangerous weakness were rewarded for their mischief-making. That they should both have voted in the House of Lords for all the measures against Clarendon, including his banishment, no doubt added an edge to his pen.

For the remaining years of the Interregnum Berkeley had nothing to fear. He had become a sacred cow. To criticise him or to call him to order would have been to jeopardise the still delicate relations between the Royal brothers. The King's servants had to grin and bear him. This was not always easy. In July 1657 Bennet obtained letters and confessions from a Cromwellian agent in Madrid which clearly showed that Berkeley's old companion-in-arms Bampfield had been active in the conspiracy between Mazarin and the Protector to divide the brothers, and that Jermyn and thus doubtless Berkeley had been privy to the whole matter.[52] This supports Carlyle's identification of Bampfield as the coded agent in Cromwell's letter to Mazarin printed above. Bennet is not an impartial witness and his source, on his own showing, is a tainted one. Did Hyde and the King accept this intelligence? We have no means of knowing. But even if they did they could hardly risk another rift with the Duke.

A month later Berkeley's indiscretion nearly led to a serious breach. Don Juan, the Spanish Commander-in-Chief, told the Duke of York in a private conversation that the King his brother had not kept his promises to him. Berkeley

---

[51] Below p. 120.

[52] *Cal. Clar. S.P.* iii, 324.

repeated this and it came to the ears of Ormonde, Hyde and the King himself who thereupon wrote to his brother to find out exactly what the accusations were. The Duke denied the report but privately explained that he did so because the remarks had been made in confidence. 'Indeed,' wrote Hyde to Ormonde, 'we are in an ill condition by the liberty Sir John* takes, and truly it will be an unreasonable restraint, if he may take that freedom to publish things to our disadvantage, and when somewhat should be done for our vindication, the case requires so much secresy, that no more words must be made of it.'[53] In September Hyde told his old friend Secretary Nicholas, no doubt ironically, that Berkeley was 'living with the Court at Brussels with all imaginable grace and sweetness; his business is a project to send the Duke of York to the Diet, but he has a thousand projects without head or foot'.[54] Even Bennet, far away in Madrid, was amused to hear of their rapprochement and wrote to the King that he did not expect it would last.[55]

At the Restoration and in the years that followed Berkeley was certainly, as Clarendon indicates, rewarded beyond any reasonable computation of his services. After this Character was written he was made, in 1670, Lord Lieutenant of Ireland. After Clarendon's death he was sent, in 1675, as joint ambassador to negotiate the Treaty of Nimeguen but the apoplexy foreseen in the sketch of him prevented him from taking any effective part. He died in 1678 at Twickenham where his memorial may still be seen in the parish church adjoining the house that had been Clarendon's country retreat from Windsor or Hampton Court.

The concluding sketch – perhaps caricature would be more accurate a description – of Arlington is the crudest. The rage

---

* The patent for his peerage was not issued till 19 May 1658.

[53] ibid. 336, 346; Clar S.P. iii, 357.

[54] Cal. Clar. S.P. iii, 360.

[55] ibid. 377.

that animates it is obvious. There is no attempt at justice and less than none at charity. The large-mindedness, the comic sense, the subtle observation of psychological detail that make the study of Bristol a masterpiece are nowhere to be seen. Instead it exemplifies the sterility of hatred.

More's the pity, because Arlington was manifestly an interesting man and Clarendon had had quite exceptional opportunities of observing him. They had first met in Oxford in the early months of the Civil War when Henry Bennet, as he then was, had managed to attach himself to the service of the brilliant Lord Digby. We may guess from what Clarendon says about Digby's stinginess and Bennet's skill in flattery that the arrangement was honorary. None the less it paid off handsomely. Bennet gained admission not only to the Court but to the intimate circle of trusted and familiar royal servants. He was sent off to Ormonde in Ireland with messages from the Queen. On his return he enlisted as a volunteer and saw action at Andover in the autumn of 1644. The sword-cut he there received was prominently commemorated for the rest of his life by the black patch on his nose. Travel in France and Italy developed his talent for languages, which even Clarendon sourly concedes, and brought him once again into the orbit of the Digby family, in this case George Digby's cousin, Sir Kenelm, who was in Rome as Henrietta Maria's chancellor and personal envoy to the Pope. About the time of the second Civil War Bennet rejoined the Queen's court in Paris and it was here that Clarendon next came across him on his way to the Madrid embassy in the autumn of 1649 and on his way back in the spring of 1651. Here, as in Oxford, their contact can only have been superficial. Clarendon was already a figure of importance, Bennet a clever and pushful young man who had held no office.

But when, at the end of that year, Clarendon was recalled to Paris by Charles II, fresh from his escape from England, the two men became distinctly aware of each other. The circumstances of their acquaintance were hardly propitious to friendship. Clarendon's loyalty to the Church of England as by law established and to the Parliamentary monarchy that claimed the same prescription was constant and absolute. He had shewn the King and the Queen that he would not compromise his principles to please them. And having taken this stand he grew more and more hostile to those who argued that everything was negotiable. These people, in his view, were the curse of the Stuart cause from first to last. The low selfishness of their motives corrupted and dishonoured their counsels. Places, possessions, titles were what they were after, in short the politics of the pig trough.

Of this school Bennet, like Berkeley and many more, was an obvious member. Starting court life as a protégé of the Queen he had moved at her initiative into the household of the Duke of York where Berkeley's position blocked his own promotion and irritated his jealousy. Recognising that the King himself must be the fountain of future rewards he had, both in the view of Clarendon and of the Duke himself, set himself to spy on one brother in order to gain ground with the other. Such mischievous ambition was, in the fragile condition of the Royalist cause, unpardonable. But Bennet's adroitness, his ease, his charm, his intelligence, his freedom from moral seriousness, were congenial to the King. The first steps to Clarendon's overthrow in 1667 were already being taken in the early 1650s.

On the personal level Clarendon's antipathy was even stronger than the political. Bennet's love of luxury was admitted to be inordinate even by those who admired his taste and enjoyed his conversation as John Evelyn did. In the penury of the Parisian exile smartness and high living were scorned by Royalists who had given up great posssessions. Lord Crofts, Bennet's cousin, was one of the handful of émigrés who felt no shame in preferring their own comfort to the sacrifices that all the others had made to the cause. He even maintained a country house near Paris to which the King went to recuperate after a serious illness. Bennet was never a man to act out of character; and it would have been out of character for him not to have made the most of this connexion. When he obtained his own establishment as ambassador to Madrid in 1657 he incurred Clarendon's censure for his too magnificent style of life.[56] This, combined with an excessive formality of manner noted by other observers such as Pepys, exasperated Clarendon's sharp resentment of anything that smacked of fraudulent pretension to rank. For him, rank was not the guinea-stamp, but the guinea itself. To falsify it was to debase the currency of society. Conscious of his own position as the son of a minor country gentleman and not unmindful of his own achievements and of his services to the Crown he refused a dukedom, refused the Garter: he did not even accept a peerage until six months after the Restoration and was only promoted to an earldom in the Coronation Honours of 1661. He was not alone in censuring Arlington for ideas above his station. 'That Lord,' said Ormonde, 'expects to be treated as if he had been born with a blue ribbon, and forgets Harry Bennet that was but a very little gentleman.'[57] Resentment was no doubt intensified by jealousy. Bennet's social origins and early career were in some respects like Clarendon's own. Both were younger sons sent to Oxford to qualify themselves as clergymen so that they could be presented to a family living. Clarendon had been nominated, but not elected, to a demyship at Magdalen (a grievance that still rankled half a century later); Bennet had come up to Christ Church with a closed scholarship from Westminster. Neither won any academic distinction but both were thought clever and witty young men. Both were snatched by events from a peaceful progress to a country parsonage for which neither would have been well suited and found themselves riding the surf of the Civil War.

What had made for jealousy could equally have made for an alliance. Clarendon and Arlington were far and away the most cultivated, the most intelligent and the best informed of

[56] See below p. 132.
[57] Carte *Ormond* iv, 693.

those leading ministers of Charles II who had served him through the long years of exile. Arlington, nothing if not pliable, would surely have worked with and not against the Chancellor if he had invited his partnership. The hostile initiative lay with Clarendon. This is confirmed both by his actions, such as denying Arlington the Post Office and, later, the Paris Embassy, and by the gross misrepresentation in the Character here reprinted. Against Clarendon's assertion that Arlington's knowledge of foreign literature was 'wholly in conversation and romances, without ever having read one serious writer' may be brought John Evelyn's description: 'My Lord . . . reades much, having both the Latine, French & Spanish tongues in perfection . . . My Lord has a library at *Euston* full of excellent bookes . . .'. The same authority refutes the allegation that Arlington 'never made a noble friendship, nor ever loved a man of clear fame and reputation, except he was of such an inferior quality, as would absolutely make him at his disposal'. Evelyn, an old and respected friend of Clarendon's, freely admits to 'the many obligations & civilities I have to this noble gent'.[58] An even more conspicuous refutation might be found in Arlington's close friendship with Ormonde's son, Ossory, the truest pattern of a noble and generous nature to be found at the court of Charles II. The charges of his ignorance of foreign affairs and of his dilettante approach to the serious business of diplomacy do not deserve examination. His judgment and conduct of policy are, like those of all who have preceded or succeeded him in these responsibilities, open to criticism. But friend and foe alike insist on his minuteness, even his pedantry, in business. Clarendon's fury was blind indeed. Had he but taken aim, what hits he could have scored.

It is not hard to see why Clarendon early in 1669 reflecting bitterly on his own situation thought of Arlington as he did. He and Sir William Coventry had been the effective political agents of his dismissal and Arlington, not Coventry, was credited with urging the King to order him into exile. Arlington, as Clarendon sat writing at Montpellier, was Secretary of State, empowered to censor all Clarendon's private correspondence: Arlington, who had stood for nothing, risked nothing, had indeed weakened the cause of Church and King by pandering to Charles II's disreputable pleasures and allying himself with the frivolous and worthless company from whom he ought to have weaned him.

The conclusion of the piece states Clarendon's fundamental objection to Arlington. He had no real principles in politics or religion. And because he had none, argues Clarendon, he inclined towards the French model of absolutism in government, which left the King and his servants freer to get on with the job and to enrich themselves in the process, and towards Roman Catholicism in religion because he felt at home in Catholic countries and was in any case insufficiently interested in the subject to try to understand what Protestantism was about. Both these judgments appear well founded, the more so when Arlington's role in the Secret Treaty of Dover is considered. He did not, like his colleague Clifford, care enough about Catholicism to support the policy or understand enough about the equipoise of the Restoration to oppose it. Clarendon himself can have known nothing of it but one can imagine the horror with which he would have recoiled from the negotiation and the contempt he would have felt for a minister who simply shrugged his shoulders and allowed himself to become the instrument of it. It would have been a contempt different in quality from anything he could have felt for a man like Jack Berkeley. In spite of himself Clarendon knew that Arlington had superior abilities and had improved them by reading. He himself had read, and preserved among his papers, Arlington's letter to the King, written from Madrid on 25 September 1658 advising him to burn all his other books and read nothing but Philip de Commines and Davila.[59] There were not many besides

[59] Clar. MS 58. f. 362.

Clarendon in the King's close circle of advisers who had read either.

Arlington is so prominent a figure that every writer on the Restoration period has to take account of him. The facts of his political career have been often recited and variously interpreted. There is an excellent biography of him by Violet Barbour, written more than seventy years ago and unlikely to be superseded. It is therefore unnecessary to summarise or outline what is already well known.

The separate consideration of these four characters has led to some repetition where their paths have intersected or run parallel. From these particularities are any general themes discernible? One that can hardly have escaped Clarendon was that all four, once his companions in exile, were now peers of the realm enjoying the fruits of the Restoration that he had done more than any man to bring about. And all four, in their different ways and with their very different abilities, had been disastrous, or would have been if they had had the means to be so. Digby and the attempt on the Five Members, Arlington and the Dutch War that had undermined the precariously re-established position of the Crown, were in a class by themselves. But Jermyn's unscrupulous greed and Berkeley's ambitious meddling had raised alarming hazards. All four were courtiers by nature or by aspiration, jealous, egocentric, competitive. All four were without clear principles in religion or politics. All four would have been driven with a flaming sword from Great Tew, that garden of England's lost innocence, to which Clarendon's thoughts in his last exile so readily turned.

Richard Ollard
Norchard
May 1988

George Digby (left against the pillar) with his
future brother-in-law, William, Lord Russell,
later fifth Earl of Bedford. Van Dyck.

George, Lord Digby

LATER
2ND EARL OF BRISTOL

H E WAS OF A VERY EXTRAORDINARY COMPOSITION BY nature, and if he had not from thence had some infirmities very prevalent over him, the advantages he had in his education must have rendered him a person of rare perfection; and in truth, a person of rare parts he was. He was born in Spain,[1] in the early growth of his father's greatness, who sailed for many years with a full gale of success, till he was grown to a great height both in title and fortune.[2] In which time his son received all the benefits of all sorts, which a liberal support, and a well ordered education could bring to him; and though he made a journey or two into his own Country, yet his whole breeding upon the matter was in Spain, till he was thirteen years of age; so that that language might very well be called his own, and no Spaniard spoke it more naturally than he did ever after. When by the all disposing power of the Duke of Buckingham, his Father was not only removed from Court, but committed to the Tower, he was sent with a Petition to the House of Commons on his Father's behalf, which he delivered at the Bar, with a short speech of his own, which being delivered with confidence by a youth very young, of delicate features, and a very graceful person, made a good impression on that Body, and caused him to be looked upon as a young man of great expectation; but the same cloud of prejudice and disfavour still covering his Father, though he had his liberty, the whole family retired

into the country. His Father grew rich, and was esteemed as a
very wise man, who had sailed very prosperously, and made
a great voyage whilst the wind was with him, and when it
raged against him in terrible storms and tempests preserved
himself unhurt, and rested in greater security than his enemies;
and, it may be, his reputation and esteem was the greater for
having no favourable aspect from the Court. In this calm the
young Gentleman was sent to the University of Oxford,[3]
being excellently prepared by his youthful studies for that
approach, and from thence, after some years spent with
notable success in all kind of learning, he went into France, in
the language whereof he was well versed, and had been
carefully instructed; and after some time spent there, in a
condition liberally supported for any virtuous improvement
of himself, but not for riot or impertinence, he returned
again to his Country, and his Father's house,[4] the most
accomplished person that that nation, or it may be, that any
other at that time could present to the world, to which the
beauty, comeliness, and gracefulness of his person gave no
small lustre.

It was no small advantage to him, that the misfortune of
his Father (though such benefits are seldom grateful to those
who most enjoy the fruit of them) made his retreat and
residence in the country absolutely necessary, for he had
several temptations and inclinations in his nature, which, if
he had lived in Court, would have brought him sooner into
many difficulties which he was afterwards perplexed with,
when he was better able to struggle with them; and there
being no footing for him there, necessity made it his choice
to live in the country in his Father's house; in which he
enjoyed, besides the benefit of his Father's information, a
very liberal conversation with men of the best quality and
parts (who frequently resorted thither, as to a house where
they found very good reception) and leisure enough to intend
his books, in which he took wonderful delight, and made so
great a progress, that he was a stranger to no part of learning,
and very subtle in the most curious parts of Philosophy, and

excellently versed in the Latin and Greek Fathers, and those
controversies in which their authority is applied by all the
parties who contend. And in this time he writ a discourse to
his Cousin Sir Kenelm Digby against the Catholick Religion,[5]
which he would never afterwards take upon him to answer,
when he grew to have a better opinion of it, or a worse of his
own, than he was then thought to have; and lest this exercise
might make him be thought too grave and serious for his
age, he made it manifest that he was excellently versed in all
polite learning, and in all the Poets, Greek and Latin, so that
when a man produced a serious discourse of his of religion,
or the abstruser part of philosophy, he found commonly in
the same company somebody, who likewise produced a copy
of verses in Latin, or English, or some facetious discourse by
letter or otherwise, upon the reading some book, or lighter
argument, writ by the same pen. And in this blessed retreat
he lived, his great abilities being communicated abroad
solicitously enough, and his infirmities unknown, but to
very few, and as carefully concealed by them; nor was he
heard of at Court till a too loud, and a furious pursuit of an
amour, within the very ears of Whitehall, made him be taken
notice of, and for which (after he had chastised, rather than
fought with an insolent, but faint adversary[6] who was too
much favoured there) he was first committed to prison, and
afterwards very severely prosecuted with circumstances not
usual to persons of that quality; so that he was forced again to
retire into the country, with so much more accrimony towards
the Court, as his own particular reckoning added to his
Father's accompt; which increased more the stock of his
reputation with those who judged of men's affections to their
Country, by the disaffection the Court had for them, and the
reciprocal disesteem they had for it.

When the disorders of Scotland obliged the King to call a
Parliament, he was, by the universal election of the populous
County where he lived, chosen to serve as one of their
Knights, where his person, and his parts, and the fame and
reputation he had, made him quickly taken notice of; and the

George Digby. Painted by Van Dyck at about the
same time as the double portrait at Althorp, facing
p. 51.

conversation he chose and wedded himself to, amongst those who were resolved to find fault with every thing that was amiss, and not to be content with any ordinary application of remedies, made it easily foreseen what counsels he meant to follow; but that stage allowed so short a time for action, that no possible conclusions could be made. But a few months after, when the discontents of men were grown higher, and the reverence to the government much impaired, he being then returned again by the same people to serve in the same place, it was quickly discerned that he meant to make himself as considerable as he could. If any thing was spoken against the government more bluntly and rudely, he took up the argument and polished it, making the edge more sharp to wound than it was before, dressing the general charge with some smart instances, which made the enormity more sensible, and his delivery, and manner of speaking, from so lovely a person, and a very lovely aspect he had, was so graceful (though not altogether without affection)[7] that it wonderfully reconciled him to his auditors. When any grievances in religion were touched upon, and the government of the Church assaulted or reproached, no man improved the discourse with more bitterness and animosity, speaking of the things he would be thought to value, gravely, and as it seemed, with piety and devotion; and of the persons against whom he found it grateful to inveigh, wittily and pleasantly and scornfully; so that that party, which had the most mischievous intentions in religion, and against the Church, believed that they had gotten a Champion to their own desire, who would be equal to their stoutest adversary, even to the Bishops themselves.

The greatest combination was, and which was least communicated, the design against the Earl of Strafford, which was no sooner entered upon, and some short instances given of his exercise of a very exorbitant power in Ireland, then he entered into the argument, made him the chief author of all that was grievous in England, giving some instances of words and expressions he had used in private conversation, of a very unpopular nature, which he took upon himself to prove; which some very considerable actors in that Tragedy did often protest afterwards was the principal inducement to their hasty resolution of charging that Earl with High Treason. And from hence he grew into so entire a confidence with the other Cabal, which did not then consist of above seven or eight, that he was immediately received into the bowels of their design, and made one of those who were trusted to prepare such a charge against the Earl, that might satisfy the rest that they had done well in accusing him; and so he became quickly privy to all their secrets, knew what every particular man thought he knew, and by what means they intended to know more, what proofs they could for the present make, and how they meant to support and enlarge those truths, all their arts and artifices, which were necessary to be communicated amongst themselves, and with those Lords who were joined with them, to make their conspiracy more practicable. In a word, the whole method they proposed for their proceedings, and what they most apprehended might obstruct those proceedings, was as clearly understood by him, as by Mr. Pym and Mr. Hambden themselves.

Having now got himself to the top of the pinnacle, he began to look about him, and take a full prospect of all that was to be seen; and it is very possible, that the desperate designs of the persons with whom he had communicated, not answerable to the reputation they had of integrity to the Nation, the uningenuity of their proceeding, and the foul arts they could give themselves leave to use, to compass any thing they proposed to do; as in truth their method was first to consider what was necessary to be done for some public end, and which might reasonably enough be wished for that public end, and then to make no scruple of doing any thing which might probably bring the other to pass, let it be of what nature it would, and never so much concern the honour or interest of any person who they thought did not, or would not favour their designs: I say, possibly this observation might make some impression upon him, who without doubt had no wicked purposes himself. Let what would be the cause or the temptation, resolve he did, to steer another course, and to set up for himself upon that stock of commodities, in the getting together whereof there were so many joint sharers with him; and so he found ways easily enough (and his nature was marvellously disposed to that dexterity) to insinuate to the Court; that, if they gave him reasons for it, they might depend upon his service, and that he would make it very useful to them: and the streights they were in, and the benefit they might receive from such a promptness, bringing him such a return from thence as he could wish, he took the first occasion (before he was so much as suspected) to give his party cause to believe, that he meant not to venture himself in their bottom. As soon as there was an occasion, by the address of a great number of ministers by way of proposition, to reform many particulars both in the doctrine and discipline of the Church, he discovered his dislike of those designs and the spirit that produced them, very warmly, and because it was well known that many of those ministers had had frequent communication with him, and even consulted that very address by his consent and approbation, he took notice of it himself, and seemed much offended that they had insisted upon many particulars which he had disallowed; and so mentioned some particular expressions that had passed between them, and which offended more persons than had been privy to the conferences, and looked like a discovery of future projections which were not yet ripe.

In the public prosecution of the Earl of Strafford he continued still in the same conjunction, and kept his post amongst those who were to manage the evidence against him, but with such a temper (which could not be reasonably excepted against) that manifested enough, that he neither brought the spirit, nor would bring the testimony they expected from him, and as soon as the Trial was over, and it was discerned that the House of Peers would not take upon them the condemning the Earl, but that it would be necessary to pass an act of Parliament to that purpose, the Bill was no sooner brought into the House of Commons, but he appeared most violently against it, discovered many particulars which had passed in their most private conferences, which he said had first perplexed him, and enlarged so pathetically upon the whole matter, and against the condemning of the Earl, that that whole party had so great a detestation of him, that they had not less appetite to destroy him, than the Earl of Strafford. And this contest produced another discovery, that a very important paper, which had been produced and perused in the close Committee, and upon which they principally depended for making good their charge, had been taken away, and could never afterwards be found; and it was confidently alleged, that at the time when that paper was last seen, and lay upon the table in Mr. Pym's chamber, there were only three persons present, whereof he was one. This produced an order in the House that every one of that close Committee, who were about eight, should make a solemn protestation in the House, that he neither had that paper, nor knew what became of it. Which test he cheerfully submitted to, with the most solemn and bitter execrations that can be imagined, upon himself and his family, if he knew what was become of that paper, or if he had ever taken it away; notwithstanding which, they who were angry with him did not believe him, and confidently reported, that it was found afterwards amongst some papers of his which were taken in the house of his Father in the war, which is not probable, since it may be presumed that a man who had gotten it in such a manner, would at least, after such an enquiry was made upon it, have cast it into the fire, though there was not then any suspicion that such an action could ever have produced it.

However it was the inconvenience of that discovery, produced by the surreption of that paper, that it produced many other notable discoveries with it, which were all cast upon his accompt, who was looked upon as a deserter at least, if not a betrayer of his party; and so from as great an height of applause, and even adoration, which he had attained to by Christmas, before Easter he was fallen to so low an esteem with all that people, that they thought no reproach equal to his demerit, and prosecuted him accordingly with their utmost animosity and rage. The truth is, he had a wonderful, and a very extraordinary facility throughout the whole course of his life, to arrive sooner to a great pitch of esteem and being beloved, than any man I ever knew; and then would make the greatest haste, to fall from that estimation into a gulph of prejudice and detestation, which can be imagined; which wrought the unusual effect, that he had scarce a notable enemy throughout his life, with whom he had not held a very great friendship, or at least profest such an inclination to, which, in any other man, would have amounted to friendship, and he bore both the extremes very unconcernedly, imputing the first to his own virtue, and transcendant parts, and his dexterity in managing them; and the latter, to the unsteadiness and inconstancy of other men's humours, to their envy and jealousy of his master faculties.

He was now compelled to transplant himself into the Court, when the soil was neither so fruitful, nor the air so pleasant as it had formerly been; indeed, where a nipping frost had induced a marvellous sterility, and in this too his constitution was so happy that he found a consolation for himself, and industriously imputed that to his generosity and election, which other men thought to be the effect of his necessity, and that he could grow no where else, when he endeavoured to grow there. It was a very melancholy season there, where most of those who had received the greatest obligations from their master, and were most able to have done him service, not only forsook him, but betrayed him; and in order to getting credit with those who suppressed all other authority, they discovered all they knew which might advance the evil designs of the other, with whom they resolved to go thorough sharers in all that was to be gotten; and the other few who retained still their fidelity and their zeal, with indignation enough to see the backsliding of their fellows, were yet so terrified with the power of the other, and with the perfidiousness that they saw every day practised, insomuch as nothing was said or done in the most secret places of the Court, even by the King or Queen themselves, but it was communicated to those who had no modesty in the considering it, but impudently declared that they would remove all persons from the King and Queen, whose very looks were not grateful to them, of which they had already given many instances. So that they, who, I say, wanted not faith, were yet without skill to foresee what they were to do, and the King himself found his infelicity to be so monstrous, that he knew not with whom to advise, nor in truth whom to trust; for they, who had no mind to betray him, were betrayed themselves, and out of their trusting others, made themselves accessary to the betraying him. In this conjuncture, the vivacity of such a person could not but be very acceptable, who had a brain perpetually working, and a conception and understanding deliberating and resolving together, and a courage so keen and fearless, that he was ready to execute the same minute whatsoever was resolved. The truth is,

> Si duos præterea tales Idæa tulisset
> Terra viros[8]

God only knows what might, or might not have resulted from his bold temper; when the party, that did all the mischief, was made up of those whose despair of being safe any where else, and belief that the King would yield to any thing that should be confidently demanded, had thrown into that stronger side. He could no longer act upon the stage where he had so long flourished, and where his mercurial temper was not grateful, even to those to whom the violence and ill designs of the others was visible, and equally odious; so that he was called up by writ to the House of Peers,[9] as fit to move in that sphere, where he no sooner came than he gave fresh life and vigour to it, the real temper of that House retaining a vigorous affection to the King, Church, and Government, and consequently very inclined to follow his example, and to be swayed by his reason, who always delivered himself with notable advantage, and was now known to be trusted by the Court, and so like to carry on their designs in the method prescribed there, and where he was looked upon, not as having deserted his principles or his party, but as a prudent discoverer of their exorbitant designs contrary to the principles they owned, and had so retired himself from their dangerous conversation and lost their confidence, because he would not part with his innocence.

And truly, if the too great activity and restlessness of his nature would have given him leave to have sat still, and expected, and made use of those advantages, which the hasty and choleric humour of the House of Commons was ready every day to present to them, and which temper was the utmost extent of courage the House of Peers could be carried to, which did not yet suspect the designs of the worst men to be so monstrous as they shortly after appeared to be, it is very probable, the wisdom and temper of the one House, with the concurrence it would have found from the major part of the other, which was far from being corrupted, would have prevented those calamities, which, under the specious authority of the Parliament, were afterwards brought upon the Kingdom. But his nature was impatient of such repose, and he always embraced those counsels which were boldest and most hazardous, which he thought would give a greater lustre to his wit and conduct. And this unhappy infirmity and vanity made him always reserved to those with whom he most intimately consulted, and without whose concurrence he pretended to resolve nothing. Yet in any determination that was ever made between them, he always reserved some such important particular to himself, which would in truth have changed the whole Council, and have made them all protest against that which he resolved to have done, as a matter mutually adjusted between them; which he did not do out of jealousy and distrust of the other, or a contradiction of their opinions and judgment, which he was still most ready to comply with, and was upon any debate the most easily persuaded to depart from his own inclinations of any man I ever knew of such a talent in understanding, but the other reservation proceeded only, first, from an opinion that if he should communicate it, it would find a general approbation (as he was very indulgent to himself in believing that what appeared reason to him would appear so to every body else) and then the reserving it would keep somewhat for credit and reputation to himself, which was unthought of by the rest; and by this unlucky temper in his nature, many desperate inconveniences fell out to the King and to himself, which would have confounded any other man in himself, as well as with others. But such accidents were so far from making such impression upon him, that he was the more ready to embrace a new enterprize, when the old miscarried, and was the only man I ever knew of such incomparable parts, that was never the wiser for any experience or misfortune which befell him; but was as ready to take the same measures, and pursue the same expedients, often times to employ the same persons by which that miscarriage and those misfortunes had befallen him, which proceeded from a notable sagacity and confidence in himself, towards whom he never could entertain the least jealousy.

This inconvenient presumption was the longer from being discovered or taken notice of, except by a few of his most intimate friends, by the wonderful faculty he had of dissimulation, which was so profound, that he appeared the most offended and enraged when he saw any thing done that was notoriously disliked, and bitterly inveighed against the authors of those counsels which himself alone had contrived, and to the execution whereof no man else was privy. So when he had prevailed with the King to cause the Six Members to be accused, and had undertaken to cause them to be committed, when he found in the House of Peers the general disapprobation and dislike of it, he stood himself up and spake against it, and whispered the Lord Mandeville in the ear, that the King would be undone if he did not publickly discover those who had given him that counsel, and that he would immediately go to the Court and dispose him to it;

when he alone was the only man, who, without communicating it to any other, had advised that prosecution, named
all the persons, and promised the King to bring in ample
testimony and evidence against them; and all this in a season
when the King's affairs were in so good a posture, that there
was no need of such a desperate remedy, and when the heart
of the contrary party was so near broken, that they needed
such an expedient to keep up their credit and ability to do
further mischief. And therefore many sober men detested
that advice as the most visible introduction to all the misery
that afterwards befel the King and Kingdom. Yet his great
spirit was so far from failing, that when he saw the whole
City upon the matter in arms to defend them, knowing in
what house they were together, he offered the King, with a
select number of a dozen gentlemen, who he presumed
would stick to him, to seize upon their persons, dead or alive,
and without doubt he would have done it, which must
likewise have had a wonderful effect. But that counsel being
rejected, and finding his credit abated in all places, he transported himself out of the Kingdom, and was shortly after by a
wonderful retaliation of providence, and in the same method
of contempt, which he had caused to be practised towards the
other, (by publishing a proclamation to restrain them from
going out of the Kingdom, when he knew they were together
in London, and environed with a strength and power enough
to drive the King himself from Whitehall, as they shortly did)
accused of high treason, upon the most slight and trivial
suggestions, and a proclamation issued out for his apprehension; all which would have brought another man to make
serious reflections upon himself, and extinguished that
inordinate heat of brain and fancy, which had so often transported him to unreasonable and unprosperous resolutions.

But all this nothing allayed that flame, or extinguished that
fire in him, but as soon as the war broke out, or rather, as
soon as there was any appearance of it, he retransported
himself again into England, raised a regiment of horse, and
charged in the head of it at the battle of Edge-hill with as

much courage as any man, and afterwards marched with Prince Rupert towards the north; and in the way, finding the close in the city of Litchfield garrisoned by the rebels, and secured by a strong old wall and a mote, and the Prince resolving to reduce it, he caused his Foot to storm it, which being beaten off, and indeed not being sufficient in number to make such a general assault as was necessary, the other, to encourage the Officers of the Horse to make an attempt in another place, offered himself to go at the head of them, and so led them through the mote to another part of the wall which was thought to be weaker; by means whereof, and the garrison within being divided into several quarters, the Foot entered the place, and made themselves master of it with great difficulty, and with great loss, and very many of the Horse Officers who entered by the mote were killed, and the rest beaten off, himself being in the mud to the middle, and shot through the thigh with a musquet bullet, was wonderfully brought off, and afterwards recovered his wounds; but not finding that respect from the Prince which he had promised himself, he gave up his regiment of horse and retired to the Court where he was sure to find good countenance.

Though he had thus discharged himself from any command in the Army, he was always ready to engage himself as a Volunteer with it upon any brisk adventure; so he was, after the relief of Gloucester, in the pursuit of the Earl of Essex's Army, and was in the first engagement at Aubourne,[10] where he was hurt, and had all the powder of a pistol shot in his face, by which it was thought he had lost both his eyes, the bullet dropping or passing by; and the Lord Falkland being the next day killed at Newberry, he was shortly after made Secretary of State, and betook himself to the discharge of it with great intentness of mind and industry enough, and continued in that employment many years; in all which time he ran many adventures, and frequently found himself at a loss when he believed he had attained his point, and at last found the greatest part of the Officers of the Army so implacably irreconciled towards him, that he was again forced to retire from his Majesty's service with his full approbation and consent, who in truth, could not but find him, at least very unfortunate. And by degrees, after several very brisk attempts of several kinds, in which he shewed as much resolution and dexterity as could be expected from a man of great wit and unquestionable courage, he was forced to transport himself into Ireland, about the time that the Prince of Wales (after so great successes of the Rebels, and the King's Armies being upon the matter totally defeated) by his Father's command to transport himself out of England, took his first refuge in the Isle of Scilly, from whence he might naturally send to and receive intelligence from Ireland.

It hath been observed before, that the Person of whom we discourse had so rare a composition by nature and by art, for nature alone could never have reached to it, that he was so far from being ever dismayed (and greater variety of misfortune never befel any man) upon any misfortune, that he quickly recollected himself so vigorously, that he did really believe his condition improved by that ill accident, and that he had an opportunity thereby to gain a new stock of reputation and honour; and so, he no sooner found himself in Ireland (when that Kingdom was in the greatest distraction imaginable by the perfidiousness of the Irish, who having made a peace with the Marquis of Ormond the King's Lieutenant for that Kingdom, and within a few days renounced and broke it again) but he believed he was upon a stage where he should act wonders, and unite all the divided affections, and all the distinct interests, and make them all subservient to the King. The quarrel was religion, which had transported both parties to the utmost outrages of blood and animosity, which can result from that unhappy spring; and though the soberer part of the nation did really and conscientiously desire to return to their allegiance, and had thereupon prevailed so far with their general Council, that they had consented to a peace, as is said before, and which was accordingly published; yet the malignant party was so much superior and prevalent, that within few days they cancelled all that was done, imprisoned the principal persons who had contributed to that peace, and put the managery of their whole affairs into the hands of men of another temper, and committed the whole nation, and as much of the kingdom as they could dispose of, to the entire protection and disposal of the Pope, in the person of his Nuncio Rinuccini, whom he had lately sent thither, with a very large supply of arms and ammunition, to interrupt their submission to the King. He was a man of a haughty and phantastical humour and nature, with a perplexed understanding; all his faculties being disposed principally to make easy things hard, and to create intricacies out of the most clear and manifest consultations. This was the condition and posture that Ireland was in when this Gentleman arrived there, the whole kingdom being so near reduced to the obedience of the Nuncio that he seemed to have nothing to do, but to shut up the Lord Lieutenant in Dublin, till he could by a closer siege likewise subdue that capital City, and in order thereunto, he was drawing together an army from all the quarters of the kingdom. This was now a scene fit for the other's activity, and being received very kindly by the Lord Lieutenant, out of respect to his person and the character he had under the King, he quickly took upon him to say any thing in the King's name, which the Lord Lieutenant believed (for he was steered by him) might contribute to his Majesty's service in a time of so great jealousy. About the same time an express arrived from Scilly, who was sent thence to the Lord Lieutenant from the Prince of Wales, to inform his Lordship, that his Highness was newly retired to that Island, where he meant to reside as long as he should find it convenient; and because the Island was poor, and unfurnished with men, his Highness wished that he might have a hundred men sent him, with good Officers for a guard to his Person; having sent at the same time to his Royal Mother the Queen, who was then at Paris, to procure him money from thence for the support of his Person and the payment of the soldiers.

This news came no sooner to Dublin, but the person we mentioned presently conceived that the Prince's presence in

Ireland would settle and compose all the factions there, reduce the kingdom to his Majesty's service, and oblige the Pope's Nuncio, who was an enemy to the peace,[11] to quit his ambitious designs. The Lord Lieutenant had so good an opinion of that expedient, that he could have been very well contented, that, when his Highness had been forced to leave England, he had rather chosen to have made Ireland than Scilly his retreat; but being a wise man, and having many difficulties before him in view, and the apprehension of many contingencies which might increase those difficulties, he would not take upon him to give advice in a point of so great importance; but forthwith, having a couple of frigates ready, he caused a hundred men with their Officers to be presently put on board according to his Highness's desire, and the Lord Digby (who always concluded that that was fit to be done, which his first thoughts suggested to him, and never doubted the execution of any thing which he once thought fit to be attempted) put himself on board these vessels, resolving that upon the strength of his own reason he should be able to persuade the Prince, and the Council which attended him, forthwith to quit Scilly and to repair to Dublin; which he did not doubt might be brought to pass in that way that would have been grateful to the Lord Lieutenant. The Prince[12] within a fortnight after his coming to Scilly, which was in March; found the place not so strong as he had understood it to be, that the island was very poor, and that he should not be able to draw any provisions thither from Cornwall, by which commerce those Islands had still been supported, he resolved therefore, before the year advanced further, when the seas were like to be more infested with the enemy's ships to transport himself to Jersey, which he did very happily, and found it to be a place in all respects very fit to reside in, till he might better understand the present condition of England, and receive some positive advice from the King his Father.

But by this sudden remove of the Prince from Scilly, the two frigates from Dublin missed finding him there, and the Lord, whose order they were obliged to observe, made all the haste he could to Jersey, where he arrived well, and found the Prince there with many other of his Friends who attended his Highness; the two Lords being gone but the day before to attend the Queen.[13] He lost no time in informing his Highness of the happy state and condition of Ireland, that the peace was concluded, and an army of twelve thousand men ready to be transported into England, of the great zeal and affection the Lord Lieutenant had for his service, and that if his Highness would repair thither he should find the whole kingdom devoted to his service; and thereupon positively advised him, without further deliberation, to put himself aboard those frigates, which were excellent sailers and fit for his secure transportation. The Prince told him that it was a matter of greater importance than was fit to be executed upon so short deliberation, that he no sooner arrived at Jersey than he received letters from the Queen his Mother, requiring him forthwith to come to Paris where all things were provided for his reception, that he had sent two of the Lords of the Council to the Queen, to excuse him for not giving ready obedience to her commands, and to assure her that he was in a place of unquestionable security, in which he might safely expect to hear from the King his Father before he took any other resolution. That it would be very incongruous now to remove from thence, and to go into Ireland before his messengers returned from Paris, in which time he might reasonably hope to hear from the King himself, and so wished him to have patience till the matter was more ripe for a determination.

This reasonable answer gave him no satisfaction, he commended the Prince's averseness from going into France, which he said was the most pernicious counsel that ever could be given, that it was a thing the King his Father abhorred, and never could consent to, and that he would take upon himself to write to the Queen, and to give her such solid advice and reasons that should infallibly convert her from that desire, and that should abundantly satisfy her, that his going into Ireland was absolutely necessary; but that a little delay in the execution of it might deprive them of all the fruit which was to be expected from that journey, and therefore renewed his advice and importunity for losing no more time, but immediately to embark. Which when he saw was not like to prevail with his Highness, he immediately repaired to one of those of the Privy Council who attended the Prince, with whom he had a particular friendship,[14] and lamented to him the loss of such an occasion, which would inevitably restore the King, who would be equally ruined if the Prince went into France, of which he spake with all the detestation imaginable, and said, he was so far satisfied in his conscience of the benefit that would redound from the one, and the ruin which would inevitably fall out by the other, that he said, if the person with whom he held this conference would concur with him, he would carry the Prince into Ireland even without, and against his consent. The other person answered that it was not to be attempted without his consent, nor could he imagine it possible to bring it to pass if they should both endeavour it; he replied, that he would invite the Prince on board the frigates to a collation, and that he knew well he could so commend the vessels to him, that his own curiosity would easily invite him to a view of them, and that as soon as he was on board, he would cause the sails to be hoisted up, and make no stay till he came into Ireland. The other was very angry with him for entertaining such imaginations, and told him they neither agreed with his wisdom nor his duty, and left him in despair of his conjunction, and at the same time of being able to compass it.

He had no sooner discharged himself of this imagination,[15] but in the instant (as he had a most pregnant fancy) he entertained another with the same vigour, and resolved with all possible expedition to find himself at Paris, not making the least question but that he should convert the Queen from any further thought of sending for the Prince into France, and as easily obtain her consent and approbation for his repairing into Ireland; and he made as little doubt, with the Queen's help, and by his own dexterity, to prevail with

France to send a good supply of money by him into Ireland, by which he should acquire a most universal reputation, and be the most welcome man alive to the Lord Lieutenant; and transported with this happy auguration he left Jersey, leaving at the same time his two ships and his soldiers, and half a dozen gentlemen of quality, who, upon his desire and many promises, had kept him company from Ireland without one penny of money to subsist upon during his absence.

As soon as he came to Paris and had seen the Queen, whom he found very well inclined to do all she could for the relief of Ireland, but resolute to have the Prince her Son immediately with her, notwithstanding all the reasons pressed against it by the Lords of the King's Council who had been sent from Jersey, he attended the Cardinal, who understood him very well and knew his foible. He received him with all the ceremony and demonstration of respect he could possibly express, entered upon the discourse of England, celebrated the part which he had acted upon that stage in so many actions of courage and sagacity, of the highest prudence and circumspection, with an indefatigable industry and fidelity; he told him that France found too late their own error, that they had been well content to see the King's great puissance weakened by his Domestic troubles, which they wished only should keep him from being able to hurt his neighbours,[16] but that they never had desired to see him at the mercy of his own Rebels, which they saw now was like to be the case, and they were therefore resolved to wed his interest in such a way and manner as the Queen of England should desire, in which he well knew how much her Majesty would depend upon his counsel. He said it was absolutely necessary, since the Crown of France resolved to wed the King's interest, that the person of the Prince of Wales should reside in France, that the method he had thought of proceeding in was, that the Queen of England should make choice of such a person whom she thought best affected, and best qualified for such an employ-ment, whom the King would immediately send as his extra-ordinary Ambassador to the King and to the Parliament, that he should govern himself wholly by such instructions as the Queen should give him, which he knew would be his work to prepare, that all things should be made ready as soon as the Queen would nominate the Ambassador, and that upon the arrival of the Prince of Wales in any part of France, as soon as notice should be sent to the Court of it, for which due preparation should be made, the Ambassador should be in the same manner dispatched for England, with one only instruction from France, which should be; That he should demand a speedy answer from the Parliament, whether they would satisfy the demands he had made, which if they should refuse to do, he should forthwith in the King his Master's name declare a war against them, and immediately leave the kingdom and return home, and then there should be quickly such an army ready as was worthy for the Prince of Wales to venture his own person in, and that he should have the honour to redeem and restore his Father. This discourse ended, he wanted not language to extol the generosity and the magnanimity of the resolution, and to pay the Cardinal all his compliments in his own coin, and from thence to enter upon the condition of Ireland, in which the Cardinal presently interrupted him, and told him he knew well he was come from thence, and meant to return thither, and likewise the carriage of the Nuncio; that the Marquis of Ormond was too brave a gentleman, and had merited too much of his master to be deserted, and France was resolved not to do its business by halves, but to give the King's affairs an intire relief in all places, that he should carry a good supply of money with him into Ireland, and that arms and ammunition should be speedily sent after him, and such direction to their Agent there as should draw off all the Irish from the Nuncio, who had not intirely given themselves up to the Spanish interest.

The Noble Person had that which he most desired, he was presently converted, and undertook to the Queen that he would presently convert all at Jersey, and that the Prince should obey all her commands, and entered into consultation with her upon the election of an Ambassador, and what instructions should be prepared for him, which he took upon himself to prepare. Monsieur Bellievre was named by the Queen, whom the Cardinal had designed for that office; the Cardinal approved the instructions, and caused six thousand Pistoles to be paid to him who was to go to Ireland, and though it was a much less sum than he had promised himself from the magnificent expressions the Cardinal had used to him, yet it provided well for his own occasions. So he left the Queen with his usual professions and confidence, and accompanied those Lords to Jersey, who were to attend upon his Highness with her Majesty's orders for the Prince's repair into France, for the advancement whereof the Cardinal was so solicitous, that he writ a letter to the old Prince of Condè,[17] which he knew he would forthwith send to the Queen, as he did; in which he said that he had received very certain advertisement out of England, that there were some persons about the Prince of Wales in Jersey, who had undertaken to deliver his Highness up into the hands of the Parliament for twenty thousand Pistoles, and this letter was forthwith sent by the Queen to overtake the Lords, that it might be shewed to the Prince, and that they who attended upon him might discern, what would be thought of them, if they dissuaded his Highness from giving a present obedience to his Mother's commands.

As soon as they came to Jersey, he used all the means he could to persuade his friend to concur in his advice for the Prince's immediate repair into France, he told him of all that had passed between the Cardinal and him, not leaving out any of the expressions of the high value his Eminence had of his particular person, that an Ambassador was chosen by his advice, and his instructions drawn by him, from no part of which the Ambassador durst swerve, and, which is very wonderful, he did really believe for that time, that he had both nominated the Ambassador, and that his instructions would be exactly observed by him (so great a power he had always over himself that he could believe any thing which was grateful to him) that a war would be presently proclaimed upon their refusal to do what the Ambassador required, and that there wanted nothing to the expediting this great affair but the Prince's immediate repairing into France without further delay, there being no other question concerning that matter, than whether his Highness should stay in Jersey, where there could be no question of his security, until he could receive express direction from the King his Father, and therefore he conjured his friend to concur in that advice, which would be very grateful to the Queen, and be attended with much benefit to himself; telling him how kind her Majesty was to him, and how confident she was of his service, and that if he should be of another opinion, it would not hinder the Prince from going, who he knew was resolved to obey his Mother; and so concluded his discourse with those arguments which he thought were like to make most impression in him, and gave him the instructions by which the Ambassador was to be guided.

His friend, who in truth loved him very heartily, though no man better knew his infirmities, told him; whatever the Prince would be disposed to do, he could not change his opinion in point of counsel, until the King's pleasure might be known; he put him in mind, how he had been before deceived at Oxford by the Comte de Harcourt, who was an Ambassador likewise, as was then thought, named by ourselves and whose instructions he had likewise drawn, and yet he could not but well remember how foully that business had been managed, and how disobligingly himself had been treated by that Ambassador; and therefore he could not but wonder that the same artifices should again prevail with him, and that he could imagine that the instructions he had drawn would be at all considered, or pursued, further than they might contribute to what the Cardinal for the present designed; of the integrity whereof they had no evidence, but[18] had reason enough to suspect. And so neither's persuasions working upon the other, the Prince shortly removed into France, and he pursued his journey for Ireland with as much of the French money as was left, whereof the Lord Lieutenant never received one thousand Pistoles towards the support of his Majesty's affairs.[19]

When he landed in Ireland, he found the whole Treaty of Peace disavowed and made void by the Irish, under the command of the Nuncio, who was declared both General at Land and Admiral at Sea of that Kingdom. Here was a new field for action, which this person presently entered into, made a journey upon very little encouragement or security in his own person to the Nuncio, was received and entertained by him very rudely, till he found it necessary, with great difficulty, to make what haste he could again to Dublin, where he continued to have many imaginations of uniting parties and dividing the Irish amongst themselves, until he plainly discerned that there was no way left to preserve that Kingdom from being irrecoverably lost to the Crown, but by putting it into the hands of the Parliament, which still made profession of all duty to the King; and when that was unavoidably to be done, and the Commissioners from the Parliament arrived to receive it, he found means again to transport himself into France, where he immediately found himself engaged in several quarrels upon the account of what had formerly passed in England, which without any kind of scruple he appeared ready to answer with his sword in his hand, his courage having always faithfully seconded him in all his designs. When these contests were over, he repaired again to his new friend the Cardinal, who received him not with the esteem he formerly had done, and only as a man who had proposed to himself to live upon them, yet he gave him very good words, promised him some command in the Army, he proposing to himself no other course of life for his subsistence and preferment, than in the war; and in the meantime gave him a very mean supply for his present subsistence, nor did he find any better reception from those of whom he expected to be admitted as a full sharer in all they enjoyed. This mortification would have broken any other man's spirits, but it gave him only some fits of indignation, without working in the least degree upon the vigour of his mind, resolving to take the first opportunity to make himself to be more considered, and an opportunity shortly offered itself, which could have hardly been propitious to any man born under another constellation.

The disorders of Paris[20] had forced the King to retire from thence to St. Germains, and all overtures towards accommodation being hopeless, forces were raised on both sides, some of the Princes of the blood being in the head of those in Paris, and others with the King; and when both Armies were one day drawn up at a small distance from each other, the Person we are discoursing of, having with some difficulty procured a horse, had put himself as a volunteer into the King's troops, and a person of the other side coming out single out of the troops in a bravado to change a pistol (as the phrase is) with any single man who should be willing to encounter him, he, without speaking to any body, moved his horse very leisurely towards him, the other seeming to stand still and expect him, but he did in truth dexterously retire so near his own troops, that before the time he could come to charge him, the whole front of that squadron discharged all their carbines upon him, whilst the other retired into his place. By this dishonourable proceeding he received a shot in the thigh with a brace of bullets, and keeping still his horse, needed no excuse for making what haste he could back, when he could no longer sit his horse.

This action being performed so gallantly in the view of the King, the Cardinal, and the Prince of Condé, all men enquired who the Gentleman was, and very few knew more than that he was an Englishman; but his name was quickly known and published, and direction given for his accommodation and recovery, in such a manner, as expressed that the King thought himself concerned that he should want nothing, and from this action and accident he made another glorious flight into the world, for he was no sooner recovered of his wounds, and went to make his acknowledgment to the King and the Cardinal, but he found the Cardinal's countenance very serene towards him, and himself quickly possessed of an

George Digby, soon after his succession to the
title as second Earl of Bristol, by Justus van
Egmont. He received the Garter, whose sash he is
wearing only a month or so after his father's death
in 1653.

honourable command of Horse, with such liberal appointments as made his condition very easy, the Cardinal taking all occasions to do him honour, and he very well knowing how to cultivate those inclinations.

If he had been born to be happy, or had had a temper to have received the approaches of good fortune, when she made most haste towards him, no man had ever prepared such an ascent to himself to any height he could propose; he was the discourse of the whole Court, and had drawn the eyes of all men upon him; his quality, his education, the handsomeness of his person, and even the beauty of his countenance (being not at that time above thirty years of age, and looking much younger) his alacrity and fierceness in action against the enemy, his softness and civility in all kind of conversations, his profound knowledge in all kind of learning, and in all languages, in which he inlarged or restrained himself, as he saw opportunity, made him grateful to all kind of persons.

His first troop of Horse consisted most of English, who resorted to him in as great numbers as he could wish, and who thought their fortunes made by their dependance upon him; and he was well contented they should do so, not concealing any imagination of his own of the vast height his stars would carry him to, imputing still all success to his own rare contrivance, and dexterity in the management, and encouraged them to hope all for fortunes under his conduct, which brought great joy and satisfaction to them both; they, congratulating with themselves for the great blessing that had befallen, that they had committed their fortunes into the hands of a person who could so easily, and was resolved so amply to provide for them, and so they celebrated him in all places as the wonder of the world; and he, too much delighting in that kind of celebration, requited them only in giving them equal testimony as brave men, excellent officers, who having the choice of all offices and preferments, made it their choice, out of their mere love and esteem of his person, to grow up under his shadow, and in the mean time that they would wait with patience and industry that they might take their turn with him. But patience and industry were virtues that neither of them were acquainted with, they were pleased with him because his professions and promises were very early, and so like preferments, that they concluded, that he that said more than they could wish in the first and second weeks, would give them possession of something within three or four months. And he again believed that all their professions and zeal proceeded purely out of an innate affection to his person, would never be weary of their dependance, or that he should still be able to keep it warm with the same fire by which he had kindled it. So that they being men of licence and expence, who expected present liberal support, he having given them cause to expect much more, and he having not in his nature the least inclination to bounty or generosity, they grew quickly weary of each other, they abandoning him as a person who promised vastly, lightly, and unreasonably, and who would not perform, if it were in his power to do it as easily as to promise; and he looking upon it as a great advancement to his fortune to be freed from such an importunate and insatiable dependance. When he made his first Cornet for his troop, his impress was an Ostrich, which is his own Crest, and in its mouth a piece of iron, under it, these words, *Ferro vivendum est tibi, quid præstantia plumæ?*[21] – alluding to the nature of the Ostrich to live upon iron, which was now his fortune to do, without any benefit from the beauty of her feathers, as he was to expect none from the lustre of his pen, in which he believed he excelled all men. The invention had sharpness in it, and added to his reputation, even when it appeared to be full blown.

Whilst the Civil Wars of France continued, and every day discovered treachery and falsehood in the Court, amongst those who were least suspected, his credit grew to that degree, both with the Queen and the Cardinal, that he was admitted into the greatest trust, and was in truth ready for the boldest undertakings, in which he had sometime success, which he never forgot, but he never remembered want of it, or when he had succeeded very ill; and was as prepared for any new undertaking. And in truth, the changes he met with, and even the reparations he sometimes received, might well work upon a nature less sanguine than his. Upon the King's first coming to Paris after the Murther of his Father, at which time he stood possessed of the Office of Secretary of State, he had some very good friends about the young King, who did wish that he might receive all gracious treatment from his Majesty, as a man who had behaved himself faithfully and signally in the service of his Father, and being of that rank and quality as had seldom received any diminution upon the succession of the Crown. But his Majesty very quickly discovered such an aversion for him, that he did not receive him with any degree of grace, nor admit him into any kind of consultation, there being some persons of inferior condition about him who had made it their business to make the worst impression they could of him, principally infusing into him, that he was the most obnoxious person in England, and the most ingrateful to all degrees of persons, and therefore his Majesty could not do a more unpopular thing than to receive such a person into any kind of credit with him.

These and the like infusions prevailed so far, as that an obstinate aversion was too easily discovered by those who stood very near, and he himself discerned it soon enough not to expose himself till it was discerned by others at a farther distance; and therefore he speedily withdrew himself from any further attendance, and retired to his command in the Army, where he grew every day, and where he pleased himself with the having discharged his duty in the overture of his service, and as much, that that overture was rejected, the acceptance whereof might have made him less solicitous to have prosecuted his fortune, which providence had laid before him, in a more specious way. And in his resentments of this kind he was naturally very sharp and flowing, let the persons be of what quality soever which were to be mentioned upon those occasions; and yet within two or three years,

together with the progress he made in the war, he recovered
so much credit with the person of the King, by his own pure
address and dexterity, that he not only made himself acceptable to him in conversation, but so gracious, that he made
him Knight of the Order,[22] which was the greatest honour he
could bestow, and the most useful to the person on whom he
bestowed it. And here he again congratulated his stars for the
neglect and affront he had formerly sustained, and his own
genius for the honour and reparation he had wrought out for
himself by his wisdom in supporting it; and at the time when
he had this obligation conferred upon him, the King was at
the Louvre with his Mother, and the City of Paris, with
many of the Princes, in rebellion. Whilst the King and his
army were about St. Germains, he frankly undertook, by his
pretence to pay his duty to the King, that he would introduce
officers and men enough to possess himself of the Louvre,
where the King was in great jealousy and umbrage with the
Princes and the City; and when the execution of this design
was by some accident interrupted, he never thought he owed
an apology to the King for engaging in such an enterprize, in
which his person and his honour was to be so much concerned,
without so much as communicating it to himself, but would
with all assurance declare, that he ought not to let the King
know of it, because it could not be presumed he would
consent to it, and then it would be in his power to prevent it;
and therefore it ought to be done without his privity, which
would absolve him from being thought to have a hand in it,
and the advantage would be so great to the King of France's
service, and his own glory in the lustre of such an action, that
he was obliged in honour to undertake it.

His commands now were grown so considerable, not only
in point of honour, but in point of profit (the greatest part of
the trade to Paris being driven under his passes and licence,
he having the command of those rivers, by which they were
to have their entrance) that it was concluded by all men, that
he would in a very short time raise a very great estate to
himself, it being evident enough that he never dispensed

with, or remitted the least sum of money which he could exact; that he never made expence in eating or drinking; never had any expence in equipage; never exercised any thing of bounty towards friend, servant or dependant, and as little charity towards any person who stood in want of relief, of which he had worthy objects enough in many distressed persons of his own country, yet (which is the most wonderful part of his life) he was not only always without money, but without those supplies of linnen and clothes which all men were possessed of who served in a much inferior condition; all which (for it was notorious to all) men then imputed to his excess in play and gaming, in which he was exceedingly delighted, and always over-reached, for he played not well; and to some amours in which he had always the vanity to involve himself, and to which he might possibly make some sacrifices for that vanity's sake. It is very true he was in his constitution, and as much in his nature, very amorous; and whether to exercise that part of his oratory, which he thought graceful and powerful in making love, or for the natural effects of it, he was very seldom without such a deity to sacrifice to, which he always performed so industriously, that he seemed to neglect all other things of the world. He would admire and extol the person he adored beyond what any of the poets had used to do, and then grieve and lament, and bewail his own want of merit, and unworthiness, even in tears, at his mistress's feet, making all the promises and vows imaginable, and would procure letters of his wife's desperate sickness of some disease that could not be cured, nor supported above two, or three months, and thereupon make offers and promises of marriage with the same importunity as if the time were ready for contract; and when either success, or want of success, had put an end to, or allayed the fervour of these addresses, he was as ready and solicitous in any new embarcation, and would act as romantic exploits as are recited in any of the romances.

Whilst he was a votary to a lady of noble extraction and incomparable beauty[23] in Paris, it happened that a young

Abbot frequented the same house, and found his presence less agreeable than he had formerly thought it had been, and had thereupon used some expressions, according to the custom and liberty of that nation and that people, which the lady thought herself disobliged by, and complained of it to many persons of quality who used to be in her presence. This noble lover being once well informed where the Abbot was, and what journey he intended to make, sent an officer that he could trust with some horse and took him prisoner, and sent him to the lady with a letter, that if he made not an entire and humble satisfaction to her for his miscarriage, he had appointed the Guard to bring him to him, and he should thereupon do such further justice as was fit. The lady was infinitely surprized and scandalized with the reparation, caused the Abbot immediately to be dismissed, without seeing him, and signified her desire to the Officer that his Superior would meddle no more in her interest, or any thing relating to her reputation; and so the matter ended, with the general laughter of the Court, it being in a time when greater extravagancies could not be examined and punished. This wonderful humour continued with him to his age, and I believe will part with him last of all his good qualities, for he is not more pleased with any, and owns this passion, when he meets with an object worthy of his address, with the same fervour and importunity, with the same languishing and tears, which he hath found benefit by near forty years, and therefore practises it with the same assurance.

When the Cardinal was compelled to leave the Court and the Kingdom, he left this person in great trust with the Queen, who took all occasions, by frequent conferences with him, and frequent testimonies of his parts and abilities, to express a very good and particular esteem of him, which he (according to the kindness he naturally had for himself) interpreted to proceed from his own great merit and abilities, which had rendered him very gracious to his Majesty; and thereupon began to delight himself with the contemplation of the glorious condition he should be possessed of, if he could now succeed the Cardinal in the Office of Primier[24] Minister in France. And this transported him so far, that he was not only well contented with the universal jealousy and clamour against the Cardinal's return, but bare-faced took upon himself to advise the Queen not to affect it, as a thing impossible to be brought to pass, and that the very desiring it would expose her own security to great hazard; which she no sooner perceived (though with a countenance of grace) than she gave the Cardinal advertisement of it, that he might incur no further inconvenience by that trust; and the other found himself insensibly deprived of all further opportunities to give any counsel, and was shortly after sent with his troops into Italy in an enterprize which was not intended for success, and as soon as he returned from thence, upon pretence of State, and with many compliments from the Cardinal, in the assignation of monies to be paid to him (though not half of what was in truth due upon his appointments) he was cashiered of all his commands, and obliged to depart out of France and not to return thither, leaving behind him the reputation of a very extraordinary person, wonderfully qualified for speculation, but somewhat defective in reducing those speculations into practice.

Magnis tamen excidit ausis.[25]

Being now to begin the world again, he repaired into Flanders to the King, pretending that he had brought enough with him to support him a year, which was four times more wealth than any person about his Majesty could pretend to, and was indeed much more than he had any view of; for within less than six weeks he had spent all that he brought from France, and therefore he bestirred himself betime for early ways of supply. He staid very few days with the King at Brussels, but the army being then in the field and under the command of Don Juan, he repaired speedily to him. His friends, who wished him very well, despaired that he would find any good reception there; it is very true he had the language of a Spaniard, having been born, and lived many years in Madrid, as hath been said before, but the gaiety of his humour, and his whole behaviour was most contrary to the nature of Spain; besides he had in his whole comportment, both in France and Italy, rendered himself very ungracious to that whole nation. Don Alonzo de Cardinas, who was in principal trust about Don Juan, had lived very many years in England, knew the other gentleman very well and the universal reproach he lay under there, and how unsuccessful his fine mercurial temper had always been in the forming any solid counsels, and therefore he was like to use all his credit to obstruct his pretences. Lastly, he had commanded a party of horse and dragoons a year or two before, in a winter expedition upon Flanders; which was the most famous for plunder and all kind of rapine, and for the unnecessary conflagration of many villages and towns, that had been in that whole war. So that his name had been rendered most odious in lampoons and songs throughout that whole province; all which, together with the streights and necessities the Spanish affairs at that time were in, and the insupportable poverty both of the Army and the Court at that time, would have discouraged any other man from that application; but all this rather sharpened than abated his edge, and after he had stayed three or four days at Brussels with the King, and entertained his Majesty with variety of pleasant discourses concerning France and Italy, especially the great expressions the Cardinal used to him at parting, when all mistakes were cleared and a new friendship entered into between them, he made his journey to Don Juan, who was then with his army before Condè, without any other advantage or credit than the strength of his own genius; for he carried not with him so much as any recommendation from the King, nor desired it.

His reception at the army was with state and reservation enough, as a man towards whom they meant to stand upon their guard. In the mean time he, according to his natural vivacity, made all his addresses as well to the Ministers and Officers, as to Don Juan, as was most proper to their several tempers and humours, in which he prevailed so far over Don

Alonzo's own parched stupidity, and commending his great
abilities in State affairs (in which he was invincibly ignorant)
that he thought he had not well enough known him before,
and wished he might have credit enough with Don Juan and
the Marquis Carracina,[26] that he might be believed in the
testimony he gave of him. In very few days he had made
himself so acceptable to all kind of persons, that he was
generally looked upon as a very fine gentleman, and of
extraordinary parts, and Don Juan himself was very well
pleased to see him frequently, and especially at those seasons
when he was most vacant to discourse, as at meals and in the
evening hours, in all which seasons the other attended very
diligently, entertaining him upon all subjects with very acute
and refined speculations. That Prince had very fine natural
parts, and had been very conversant in many parts of polite
learning, and more with books than that nation used to be,
and was very much superior to any person of what quality
soever who was about him, so that he quickly made it
manifest, that he was exceedingly delighted to exercise those
talents in the conversation of a person so excellently endowed
in all parts of literature.

In the time Don Juan had spent in Italy, he had been,
according to the genius of that nation, inclined to examine
the art of astrology, and was not without a greater opinion of
it than he publicly owned. The other had really waded as
deep into the examination and study of it, as any man had
done; and though he would make many pleasant discourses
upon it, and upon the general incertitude of it, yet he had in
truth a greater esteem and dependence upon it, than he was
willing to be thought to have, and had many discourses of the
observations he had made in Italy, of the great confidence
that people had in all their affairs and counsels upon those
predictions, of the success whereof he would give many
instances; and his late General the Duke of Modena[27] had
much improved his curiosity and knowledge in that science.
This argument did not only take up much of the time Don
Juan spent in public discourse, but disposed him to many

private conferences with him, until in the end, Don Juan desired him to examine his horoscope which he delivered to him, and the other as willingly received, and undertook the charge; and from this kind of intercourse which in the beginning had no other foundation, it was upon the sudden believed that the Prince held other conferences with him upon matters of greater importance, and that he had credit enough with him to prevail in many cases. So that many persons of all conditions applied themselves to him, to promote their pretences to the Prince, in reception whereof he was not forward; yet took care to cultivate those imaginations concerning his interest in the Prince, of which he intended, as he shortly after did, to make some use.

When he had raised this opinion of his parts and abilities, his next work was to manifest his interest, and the power he had to do them service. There were many regiments in the French army, which consisted intirely, both Officers and Soldiers, of Irish, some whereof during his Majesty's residence in France, withdrew themselves from the Spanish service, declaring that they would always serve their own King, or in such places as he required them. And they were now as ready to leave that Crown and to engage for the Spaniard in Flanders, to which they were the more disposed at this time, by the general rumour (which was known to be well grounded) that the Duke of York would be shortly obliged likewise to retire himself out of France, by some obligation the Cardinal was engaged in, upon his Treaty with Cromwell; and then it was reasonably enough concluded that his Royal Highness would repair into Flanders to the King his Brother, where the Duke of Gloucester already was, having found it necessary not to remain longer with his Sister in Holland, where his presence was not grateful to those States.[28]

The Spaniards having entered into a secret Treaty with the King, had permitted him to make his abode in Flanders, which was confined to the City of Bruges, rather as a Prince incognito than as a King whose quarrel and interest they had wedded. As soon as they were engaged before Condè, finding

that there were some Irish Regiments in that garrison, they
sent to the King to desire him that his Majesty would send
the Marquis of Ormond to the Camp, to the end that by his
pretence some of the Irish in the garrison might be wrought
upon, the which his Majesty consented to and sent the
Marquis accordingly, of which Don Juan found the benefit;
for the jealousy the garrison had of the Irish, made the French
Commander and Governor treat the sooner upon the surrender; and though the Lord Muskerry, who was Nephew to the
Marquis of Ormond, and commanded a strong Regiment of
Irish in that town, positively refused to bring over his
Regiment to the Spaniard upon the surrender of Condè,
which he conceived would not be honourable for him to do,
yet he declared to his Uncle, that as soon as he came into
France with his men, he would repair to the Court, and bare-
faced demand from the Cardinal a safe conduct for himself
and his men to march into Flanders, according to the stipu-
lation agreed between them, That whenever the King should
require his service, he should have a pass to march to him
with his whole Regiment; that when he had done his part,
and the Cardinal should refuse to comply with his engagement, he would take himself to be at full liberty, and would
with all speed repair to his Majesty, and made no doubt but
that his Regiment would quickly find themselves with him,
which fell out accordingly; and after the Cardinal had endeavoured by all the ways he could to dispose and persuade
him to continue in that service with great promises of reward
and preferment, finding at last that he could not be wrought
upon, he gave him a licence for his own departure, but
refused to licence his men, saying, That they were readier for
the King of England's service whilst they remained in France,
than if they went into Flanders. Whereupon Muskerry himself, with his servants and equipage only, repaired to Brussels,
where he was received with great applause, both the Colonel
and the Regiment having made themselves very signal in
very remarkable services, and Don Juan no sooner assigned
him quarters for the reception of his men, but the whole

Regiment by tens and twenties repaired with their arms to him, insomuch that there were not above one Officer and very few private Soldiers who were not present with him, and there they continued till the making of the peace.

About the same time, and towards the end of the campaign, there was a strong garrison fixt and possessed by the French at St. Gillen,[24] within five mile of Brussels, under the command of Monsieur Schomburgh, who, having been possessed thereof by the space of above a year, had with great pains and care made it very strong, and was a thorn in the side of Flanders, and exceedingly discommoded their whole affairs. The Spaniard had attempted the surprize of it before it was thoroughly fortified, and made afterwards several attempts to recover it, but were always beaten off with great loss, and left hopeless of success. The major part of this garrison were Irish, whereof most of the Officers were of one family, and nearly allied to a gentleman who had long served the Marquis of Ormond in the place of a Secretary. They found means to let this gentleman know that if the King thought it would be for his service, they would undertake whenever they should be required, to put it into the Spaniard's hands. The Secretary quickly informed his Lord of the overture, and his Majesty approved that the Secretary should resort to the army, that Don Juan might know and consider the proposition, and whether it might be practicable; and the Marquis rather chose to commit the conduct of it to the gentleman who had made himself so gracious to Don Juan, than to reserve it to himself, his wisdom and his honour raising many scruples in him concerning that negociation, and he was still unsatisfied that the benefits his Majesty received from the Spaniard were not proportionable to the advantages they received from the King.

The Secretary no sooner communicated this affair to the other gentleman but he received it with open arms, and looked upon it as a thing done which his stars had contrived for the raising and establishing his fortune; he made all the promises imaginable of managing it for the particular benefit

and preferment of the Officers and Soldiers, and then communicated it to Don Juan as an affair that wholly depended
upon him, and upon the intire dependence those Officers had
upon him. The overture could not but be very grateful to
Don Juan, the reduction of that place being the most desirable
thing before them, and to be purchased at any price, and
therefore all the conditions were readily consented to, promises made for the payment of such and such sums of money
out of hand, such and such pensions to be granted upon funds
which could not be disappointed, and all other things to be
done for Officers and Soldiers which they themselves required;
and to this purpose a Treaty was entered into and signed with
all requisite formalities.

This negociation was attended with other conveniencies;
he had hitherto appeared only in the quality of a volunteer,
which title would be at an end as soon as the army retired
into their winter quarters, and he had reason to apprehend
(though there continued all fair weather in Don Juan's countenance) that the Spanish Council would not be so well
pleased to see him frequently in the Court, and in private
with the Prince, upon whose temper and inclinations he was
already thought to have some ascendant; but this affair of St.
Gillen, which was imparted to the principal Counsellers,
added infinitely to his reputation with them, and made his
presence at Brussels to be even absolutely necessary, there
being many difficulties which were in view for the execution
of the design. Schomburgh was known to be an Officer of
great vigilance and courage, and it was very probable that the
daily resort of so many Irish into Flanders, who withdrew
from the French service, would raise a jealousy of all those of
that nation who remained in that service, and therefore if the
design were not speedily executed, they must expect that the
garrison would be reinforced with other men, and the Irish
removed; and the truth is, this was in Schomburgh's purpose
from his natural jealousy of the inconstancy and infidelity of
that nation, without having discovered the least circumstance
of the Treaty. But from the time of the taking of Condè,

which administered the first suspicion of the Irish, it was not
in his power to draw new forces to him, or to dismiss those
out of his garrison whose company he least desired; thereupon he only changed one resolution he had, which was to
make a journey himself to Paris, the knowledge and time
whereof was the first ground that disposed the Officers to
this undertaking, as his presence made the work the more
difficult; but they were too many, and those too far engaged
to give over the design, and therefore the Officers within
were as solicitous for the execution of it as the Spaniards
themselves.

In the depth of winter, about Christmas, in a very great
frost and snow, Don Juan assembled all his army before St.
Gillen, with which Schomburgh was very much surprized,
and knew well that the army could do him no harm if his
men were true to him, and therefore concluded that the
enemy without depended upon treachery within, and he
quickly found by the frequent assembling of many of the
Irish Officers, and by the neglect of his orders, and sometimes changing the guards, that there was a conspiracy
against him, and that some religious men had been suffered
to pass in and out; and he intercepted one letter by which he
found the Lieutenant Colonel of the Irish Regiment of whom
he had always had a very good opinion (and he was indeed
much superior in abilities to that kind of people) deeply
engaged in the design, and indeed the whole conductor of it.
Whereupon he caused him suddenly to be apprehended, with
a resolution as suddenly to execute him, but the Officer
advised him not to make too much haste, and resolutely told
him that his own life, and the lives of all who adhered to him
should expiate for the loss of his; and in the same instant all
the Irish betook themselves to their arms, and possessed
themselves of some of the outworks, and of a place of some
strength in the town; and a trumpet was sent from Don Juan
with a letter to the Governor, in which he let him know that
he was very sure of the place in spite of all that he could do,
and therefore if he should take away the Lieutenant Colonel's

life, himself and all his friends should suffer, but if he would presently treat for the giving up of the place, he would give him conditions worthy of a soldier; in this streight the Governor found it absolutely necessary for him to treat, and quickly consented to the conditions proposed, and marched out with all those who had a mind to follow him, much the major part remaining in the Spanish service. And so Don Juan returned triumphantly to Brussels where he was the better welcome for having reduced so mischievous a neighbour in the depth of winter, which they durst not have attempted in the spring or summer.

This action so prosperously carried on gave great advantage to the affairs of that country, and the dexterous conduct of it, much reputation to the person who had been so instrumental in it, who was likewise liberally considered by the Spaniard for the service he had done, besides the consideration he took for himself out of the monies assigned for the officers and soldiers; and he now looked upon himself as settled in the service of that Crown, and in the particular affection of Don Juan, of which he made daily use. From the time of his first approach into Don Juan's good opinion, he used all the ways he could to inculcate into the King the great benefit would accrue to his service by the reputation he had gotten with the Prince and in the Spanish Councils, where he would employ all his talent and his time, to promote his Majesty's pretences; and therefore he proposed to the King, that he might be restored to the character of his Secretary, as he had been to his Father, and the place had never been yet disposed of, there being always two Secretaries of State, one of which, who had been joint officer with him, being then attending upon his Majesty,[30] and sufficient to dispatch all the business of that office.

The arguments which he used to the King to gratify him in that his desire, were, that he should be thereby enabled to do his Majesty great service by the reputation that character would give him; that he would not intermeddle with his counsels otherwise than as his Majesty should think fit to communicate them to him, in reference to the transactions which were to be made with Don Juan and in the court of Spain; that when the King should find it necessary by the advancement of his affairs in England to dispose of the place of the Secretary to a person who might merit it by any notable service, he would willingly put it into his Majesty's hands to dispose of, and betake himself to any other office he should be assigned to. By these inducements he prevailed with his Majesty to admit him into the same relation he had formerly to his Father, not at all meddling with the business of the office, nor believing that it would ever come to be an office in England, he being at that time possessed with as full a despair of his Majesty's ever being restored to his dominions, as Cromwell himself was with a confidence that it could never come to pass, and so modelling all his designs to live in a good condition abroad, in which he had hitherto prospered so wonderfully, and all places being alike and equal to him.

Hitherto he avouched nothing more than his being a Protestant above temptation, frequented the exercise of devotion in the King's house, and gave all the evidence of his affection that way as could be expected from a man who was long known to have great latitude in religion; and he had lately committed a younger son to the care and education of the Jesuits in France, upon some promise the Queen Regent had made to him when he was in credit with her, that she would provide a liberal support for him in pensions and church-livings, the receiving whereof he thought no religion could oblige a man to be averse from. Soon after his first coming into Flanders, and as soon as he found he had got credit there (which he still believed to be greater than in truth it was) he sent into England for a daughter[31] he had there, of a full growth, who lived not easily with her mother, in order by his authority to compose some domestic differences, and to finish a treaty of marriage for her with a Gentleman of the same country, who had long made that address. As soon as she arrived in Flanders, he provided a private lodging for her in Ghent, which being in the middle between Bruges, where the King resided, and Brussels, where the Spanish Court was, he thought to be a place where he could probably spend most part of his time; besides, having a great reverence for the Lady Abbess of the English monastery there, he had a particular devotion for that city; not without a design to have his own devotion the better thought of, his daughter remained very few days in the lodging he had provided for her, before he removed her to the English Cloyster for her more honourable accommodation, whilst her stay should be necessary in those parts. The young lady was as averse from a monastery and from the religion that is professed there, as is possible for a daughter who had been bred from her cradle under the severe discipline of a mother of another faith, and in an age and region where the Romish religion was perfectly detested, and she herself had always been taught very sharp objections against it; but her father easily persuaded her that there should be no attempt made upon her religion, but that the lodging should be very honourable, and the conversation such as she could not but take delight in, and that she should always be with him when he was in town, only lodge in the monastery, and eat there when he was away. And it cannot be denied but that the accommodation was very good, and prudently provided for her, the Abbess being a lady of great reputation and wisdom, and the whole community consisted of ladies of noble extraction, great beauty, and unblemished virtue; and it was a great respect in the Abbess towards her father, and her dependence upon his great power at Court that persuaded her to receive his daughter into the monastery, where none of any quality had ever been admitted into the inclosure who did not profess the Roman religion.

But she had been there very few days, when a young half-witted man of a good family and a competent fortune, meeting this young lady at some house whither she used to accompany her father, made love to her, and there being a great friendship between the Abbess and the mother of the young gentleman, who was a widow of very great reputation and esteem in that place, the matter was quickly proposed to the father, who, according to his natural alacrity, presently looked upon it as a new manifestation of providence, that he and his family should never fall to insupportable necessity, and transported with the vanity of the reputation he should acquire, that being despoiled of his estate and banished from his country, he should raise himself to such a reputation with a neighbour nation, as to marry a daughter into one of the best families of it, adorned, as he would believe, with an ample revenue, and without any other portion than a promise to pay a competent one when he should be able. Without long deliberating of the business, and without considering the weak spirit of the young man, which was in truth contemptible, or so much as examining the value and yearly revenue of the estate, which was not the twelfth part of what he himself gave it out to be; he first persuaded his daughter to renounce her own religion, and become a Roman Catholick, which was a condition without which the marriage could not be attained to, and then frankly gave her up to perpetual misery, which she entered into from the day of her marriage: which, considering all circumstances, would have brought much grief of mind to another parent, but he was of that rare constitution, that those worldly things never gave him trouble, nor did he more consider the loss of a child, in an adventure which probably might bring some convenience to him (for himself was still first, if not sole in all those considerations) than if it were his neighbour's, being absolutely divested of all troublesome affections which might obstruct or disturb his fortune, and with this kind of providence he made provision for two of his children.

Hitherto he had preserved, as he believed, his own reputation, as to being a Protestant, unblemished. He had resisted the temptations of France without being shaken, and though the Jesuits always courted him with wonderful application and observance, and he them again with the same dexterity, frequently gratifying them with some arguments against the Protestants, and acknowledging some defects to be in their church, which he could wish supplied; yet after he had lodged six months at Albey[32] in a College of the Jesuits, where he studied very hard, and read all books recommended by them to him, when the Superior came to him at his remove towards Italy, and passed many compliments with him of the honour the Society had received in entertaining so noble a person and so rarely qualified, he told him; He hoped that the observations he had made of their profession and their course of life, and the reflections which had occurred unto him upon the arguments he had found in such and such books, had by this time confirmed him in such a reverence towards the Catholick Church, that, all his former prejudice being removed, he would now throw himself into the Arms of it. He parted not with him in debt for any good words, commended the Catholick religion as containing most excellent inducements to a pious life, which could not but be attended with salvation, he admired and extolled the institution of the Society, and their strict and pious observation of the rules prescribed to them, which in his judgment made them preferable to all other religious Orders, and that he would always preserve a particular devotion for them. But he said, whether it were by the difference of their educations, or the inequality of their understandings and judgments, he found that many arguments which appeared to them as infallible demonstrations, seemed in truth to him to carry little weight with them, and so briefly enlarged upon some particular instances with a great sharpness of reason, yet with great modesty and confession of his own weakness; he concluded, that there was somewhat wanting in their religion which kept him yet from being reconciled to it, and so he took his leave of Albey.

But he now found that he must calculate his designs to another meridian, and that the temper which had done him no harm in France would do him no good in Flanders, that the reputation of being a Christian was a title sufficient for many preferments, but that not being a Catholick, in Spain took away the advantage of being a Christian. He never had any lively hopes of the King's restoration, at least that he could ever be restored but by Catholick arms, and he had just now seen the most probable design the King had ever had, upon the hope of the affection and power of his own subjects, miscarry in the attempt of Sir George Booth, which was thought to be founded upon so good mediums, that the King had withdrawn privately from Brussels incognito, and attended only with four or five servants, whereof that person was one, to the maritime parts of France, in some assurance that the Rebel's Army would find so many diversions in other parts of the Kingdom, that he should find a competent body of men to receive him in Kent, with which he might march as he should find it most counsellable. But all these high imaginations coming to nothing, by the sudden defeat of Sir George Booth before Chester, and the surprisal of many other parties in several parts of the Kingdom before they were well formed, and in a word, the imprisoning of all persons of honour and reputation throughout the whole Kingdom, who were in the least degree suspected to wish well to the King, seemed at the same time to discredit and reproach the late too easy imaginations, and to pull up by the roots all the King's future hopes of restitution, and in this melancholy discomposure of mind the King returned again to Brussels, and the other person to his retreat at Ghent to the admired Abbess and to his beloved daughter.

It was the great benefit and happiness of his constitution, that he never continued long irresolute, or remained in suspence; if that door was not open which he would chuse to enter at, the next was welcome to him. His hopes under the King were now blasted, and though he promised himself much encouragement from the favour of Don Juan, yet, as was said before, religion was that which could only make a man shine in the Court of Spain, and he had made as much of his as it would yield him throughout his whole course of life, and it was like now to do him no farther service. As soon as he came to Ghent he pretended to be very sick, sent for physicians, described his disease to them, and proposed some reasonable remedies to them; his friend the Abbess, who was really a much better casuist than her confessor, did not fail to administer her spiritual remembrances; and Courtney, the Provincial of the English Jesuits (a man who could never have been too hard for him, if he had not been reduced to great weakness) was at hand to do all his offices, and he did it very effectually, though in great secret. He sent then to the Marquis of Ormond and his other friend[33] at Brussels, upon whose friendship he had ever depended, and had found him always fast and unshaken to him, notwithstanding his many imbecillities; he conjured them both (who were indeed the two only friends he had in the world) to repair to him at Ghent, for that his condition of health being at that time so very doubtful, he had somewhat to impart to them of the last importance. The enemy had fastened themselves in some places between Brussels and Ghent, and the season of the year was not so pleasant as to invite men to unnecessary journeys, it was therefore agreed between them, that the presence of one of them would serve the turn let the business be what it would, and so the Marquis made a journey to him, the other remaining still with the King. When he came to Ghent he found him well recovered of his sickness, of which he made him a large relation; by what degrees it came upon him, and how soon it had deprived him of his strength, how his sleeps forsook him, and that the night yielded him no rest, that in his agony he had made many reflections upon his past condition of life, and principally upon some scruples in religion, which had been long in his mind, that he had sent for a learned Jesuit to confer with him, and in a word, that he had received so great satisfaction from him, that he was become Catholick, and was reconciled to the Church; which he had no sooner submitted to, but that he found so great a tranquility and serenity of mind, that he had wonderfully recovered in so few days his perfect health, and almost his former strength. That having thus provided for the salvation of his soul, all his other thoughts were for the advancement of his Majesty's service, or that at least, that this alteration in him might have no reflection upon the other, and that in this consideration he desired a conference with his two best friends; and since one of them came not, he would desire the same from the other, which he meant to do from both; that he might receive his advice how the same might be communicated to the King; and how, and when, and in what manner it should be made known; and that it was hitherto so great a secret that it was only known to his confessor and himself, and that it should remain so as long as his Majesty should think it requisite; that he had in truth himself endeavoured, as a thing practicable in his own opinion, that it might have remained so entire a secret between his confessor and himself, that he might not only have deferred making his conversion publick, but have performed all his usual offices and services about his Majesty as he had used to do, even at his devotions, so that no man should have been able to make the least discovery. But that his confessor, upon great deliberation and conference with many other very learned men, had declared to him, that what he proposed was so absolutely unlawful and inconsistent with the Catholick religion, that it was not in the power of his Holiness himself to dispense with it. This being his case, he had no more to do but to desire that the whole relation might be candidly made to his Majesty, and a gracious interpretation obtained from him upon it. The Marquis (who was less surprized than his other friend, as having less opinion of his constancy in that particular than the other had) answered him only, that he was sorry for the change, and that he should give his Majesty a full relation of it, and so returned to Brussels.

Within few days he came thither; and having been very careful to be first seen by Don Juan at Mass, he attended the King, who received him without any cloudiness, looking upon him of the same religion as he had before understood him to be. His Majesty making himself very merry with his other friend for being so weak a man as to imagine that he could be constant to any profession, and made himself no less merry with the person himself upon his scruples of conscience, and the method and circumstances of his conversion, and upon Father Courtney's having gained so great an ascendant over his understanding; and he was very glad to compound for being laughed at, and could bear a better part in it, than in the serious debate of it. He was exceedingly troubled to find his other friend, whose true affection to him had been upon all occasions so manifest, so severe that he could not dissemble it in his countenance with him; and when the other renewed all professions of kindness and friendship to him, against all persons and all pretences in the world, and desired that this alteration in him, which was the effect of conscience and for his own salvation, might not deprive him of his friendship, or alienate his affections from him, he answered him very roundly; that he could not dissemble the trouble he sustained, nor could bear that reproach which would fall upon himself if he were thought not to be displeased with it; that he knew not how he could hereafter bear any part in the King's Councils, or how he could be communicated with; that though the professions he made to him of the constancy of his friendship might be at that time according to his intention, yet that he had no reason to believe that they, who had power to prevail over him in this affair of the highest importance, would ever be contented that he should retain a friendship with a person so opposite to all their practices, and all their principles; against which they would always be able to speak more pertinently, both in reason and religion, than they had done in any other part of his conversion, which he took very heavily, and could not forbear undervaluing and envying, against the whole body of them, with more reproach and contempt, than could have been expected from so young a proselyte. The King had well foreseen that he could no longer wear the character either of his Secretary or Counseller, and it may be, that consideration had made him condescend to be so merry upon the conversion, and he was very well content that his friend should plainly declare to him in his presence, the necessity of his declining being present at future Councils, and of returning the signet to the King, with which, how much.soever he was surprized or displeased, he presently submitted, and delivered the signet the next day.

This was a change he did not expect his conversion would have produced, but had promised himself more advantage from his character in his new religion than in his old; that there was no more hope now of the Protestant Interest, and therefore that the Catholick must be now wholly applied to, and that those transactions could pass through no other hand but his, and that as the confidence of the Catholicks, should be able to advance the King's service, so his so near relation to his Royal Person and Councils would give him great credit with the Catholicks. Such a crop of imaginations and presumptions was always his first harvest upon any notable new design or enterprize, but this new exclusion demolished all these hopes, and was a greater discovery of the King's dislike of what he had done than in his calculation of State he thought seasonable for his Majesty's service, and upon that ground was the less expected by him; and this he never forgave his old friend, though he continued to make the same professions and seemed to take it very unkindly that it should be thought that religion should be able to make any impression on him with reference to the friendships which he had contracted. After the first congratulation for the becoming a Christian, which those people do very liberally make for a few days, he found no sunshine from the change of his climate, that no proffer of place, or pension came from Spain; and that the Pope, to whom he had made an early communication of his sorrow for, and renunciation of his former heresy, had returned him no other exalted expressions, which he expected, than, *Tu conversus converte fratres tuos*;[34] that Don Juan's own countenance was so far from shedding more graces towards him than it had formerly done, that it was in truth more reserved; for the Marquis of Carracina and especially Don Alonzo, who were not pleased with the frequent admission he had to Don Juan, and his serene countenance towards him, had sent their advertisements into Spain little to his advantage, and the Prince had received some reprehension from thence for his conferring those graces.

But there happened shortly after another instance, which manifested enough what opinion that Court had of him. The Treaty between the two Crowns, being appointed to be at Fontarabia between the Cardinal and Don Louis de Haro, Don Louis, who always professed great affection to the King, sent him a private advice by his Resident in that Court, Sir Henry Bennett, to find himself there, professing that he would do all he could to engage the Cardinal, that the two Crowns, being once reconciled, might both engage in his Majesty's interest, and at the same time advised that his Majesty would come with as small a train as he could fitly do, and particularly that by no means he would bring that person with him; which was a sufficient evidence of prejudice. Notwithstanding which, the Cardinal having expressly refused to grant a safe conduct to his Majesty to pass through France, and as expressly dissuaded his going to the Treaty, as a thing which would prove to his disadvantage, and disenable his Eminence, by the noise of it, to do those good offices for his Majesty which he was resolved to do in his absence, the King thought fit to follow the advice of the other favourite, and to make a journey thither though France incognito. And to that purpose he made choice of four or five servants to attend him; and though he liked very well that gentleman's company in those jolly journeys, yet at this time, the intimation he had from Spain, and the knowledge he had of the Cardinal's particular and irreconcileable displeasure towards him, made him plainly discern that it was by no means fit to have him with him. However the other in the end prevailed so far with him, for the experience he had of the ways and places through which they were to pass, that he was admitted to attend, together with the Marquis of Ormond, Daniel O'Neale, and three other servants; and in that manner they went from Brussels with all the secrecy imaginable, nor was it known in many days after whether the King was gone.

The King was contented to see as many considerable places as were within any distance of the ways through which they were to pass, and the other, who was the sole conductor, led him so far about, that the Treaty was upon the matter concluded before the King came to the borders; and then, upon the general intelligence that the Treaty was at an end, and Don Louis returned to Madrid, though the King had sent the Marquis of Ormond directly to Fontarabia to know the truth, and to inform Don Louis of his Majesty's arrival, yet without staying for his return, the other persuaded the King, that he ought to make all possible haste to Madrid, and so far prevailed, that they went as far as Saragosa in the Kingdom of Arragon, where they received clear information that Don Louis remained still at the place of the Treaty. And within a day after, an express arrived from thence, with all the importunity from the Marquis of Ormond and Sir Henry Bennett, that his Majesty would make all possible haste thither, signifying further the prejudice he had suffered by the delays he had made in his journey, and the unexpressible displeasure Don Louis had conceived upon his purpose of going to Madrid, which in that conjuncture would have occasioned great disorder in the King of Spain's affairs, all which made deep impressions in his Majesty, and made him discern how inconvenient the fanciful humour of his guide had been to him. The King's reception at Fontarabia, and his treatment there, was agreeable to the Spaniard's custom in those occasions, full of respect and application to his Majesty; and in the short stay he made there, the other person (who was upon all the disadvantages mentioned before) had by his pure dexterity and address, wrought himself so far into the good opinion of Don Louis and the other Grandees who accompanied him, that when the King returned through France for Brussels, he found encouragement to go directly for Madrid, where he was well received by the King, and supplied with at least two or three thousand pound sterling, and stayed there until he heard of the great change of affairs in England, and of his Majesty's reception there, where he found him in the full possession and administration of his Regal power.

By this time the King was engaged very far in his treaty

with Portugal for the marriage with the Queen, all particulars being in the truth upon the matter agreed upon, which no sooner came to this gentleman's knowledge but he expressed a marvellous dislike of it, and (without any capacity which might entitle him to that presumption) suggested all things to the King which the Spanish Ambassador could suggest to him, and which were most like to make some impression upon his Majesty; such as the deformity of her person, the number of her years and her incapacity of bearing children; and at the same time made offer of the choice of two young Ladies of the house of Medici, of such rare perfection in beauty as his fancy could describe, and (which is very wonderful) prevailed so far privately with the King, to send him incognito into Italy to see those Ladies, with a promise not to proceed further in the treaty with Portugal till his return, but upon a short reflection upon the dishonour of this design, his Majesty put a quick end to it, renewing his old observations of the humour and presumptions of the man. How many extravagant propositions and designs he afterwards run into, till he so far provoked the King that he gave orders for his apprehension and commitment to the Tower, is known to all men; and how many more he is like hereafter to fall into of the same kind, can hardly be foreseen, even by those who best understand his unlimited ambition, and the restlessnesss of his humour.

I did not intend to have reflected upon so many particulars, much less to have taken any survey of the active life of this very considerable person; but it was hardly possible to give any lively description of his nature and humour, or any character even of his person and composition, without representing some instances of particular actions; which, being so contradictory to themselves, and so different from the same effects which the same causes naturally produce in other men, can only qualify a man to make a conjecture what his true constitution and nature was; and at best it will be but a conjecture, since it is not possible to make a positive conclusion or deduction from the whole or any part of it, but that another conclusion may be as reasonably made from some other action and discovery. It is pity that his whole life should not be exactly and carefully written, and it would be as much pity that any body else should do it but himself, who could only do it to the life, and make the truest descriptions of all his faculties, and passions, and appetites, and the full operation of them; and he would do it with as much ingenuity and integrity as any man could do, and expose himself as much to the censure and reproach of other men, as the malice of his greatest enemy could do; for in truth he does believe many of those particular actions, which severe and rigid men do look upon as disfigurings of the other beautiful part of his life, to be great lustre and ornament to it; and would rather expose it nakedly to have the indiscretion and unwarrantable part of it censured, than that the fancy and high projection should be concealed, it being an infirmity that he would not part with, to believe that a very ill thing subtilly and warily designed, and well and bravely executed, is much worthier of a great spirit, than a faint acquiescence under any infelicity, merely to contain himself within the bounds of innocence; and yet if any man concludes from hence that he is of a fierce and impetuous disposition, and prepared to undertake the worst enterprize, he will find cause enough to believe himself mistaken, and that he hath softness and tenderness enough about him to restrain him, not only from ill, but even from unkind and ill-natured actions.

No man loves more passionately and violently, at least makes more lively expressions of it; and that his hatred and malice, which sometimes brake out from him with great impetuosity, as if he would destroy all he dislikes, is not compounded proportionably out of the same fiery materials, appears in this, that he would not only, upon very short warning and very easy address, trust a man who had done him injury to a very notable degree, but even such a man, as he himself had provoked beyond the common bounds of reconciliation; he doth not believe that any body he loves so well, can be unloved by any body else; and, that whatever prejudice is contracted against him, he could remove it if he were but admitted to conference with them which own it. No man can judge, hardly guess, by what he hath done formerly, what he will do in the time to come, whether his virtues will have the better and triumph over his vanities, or whether the strength and vigour of his ambition, and other exorbitances will be able to suppress, and even extinguish his better disposed inclinations and resolutions, the success of which will always depend upon circumstances and contingencies, and from somewhat without, and not within himself. I should not imagine that ever his activity will be attended with success or security, but without doubt, if ever his reflections upon the vanity of the world dispose him to contemn it, and to betake himself to a contemplation of God, and nature, or to a strict and severe devotion, to which he hath sometimes some temptation, if not inclination; or if a satiety in wrestling and struggling in the world, or a despair of prospering by those strugglings, shall prevail with him to abandon those contests, and retire at a good distance from the Court to his books and a contemplative life, he may live to a great and a long age, and will be able to leave such information and advertisements of all kinds to posterity, that he will be looked upon as a great mirror by which well-disposed men may learn to dress themselves in the best ornaments, and to spend their lives to the best advantage of their country.

Sir John Berkeley, first Lord Berkeley of Stratton.
Artist unknown.

SIR JOHN BERKELEY

LATER
LORD BERKELEY OF STRATTON

HE WAS A MAN OF A TEMPER AND CONSTITUTION WHICH made him incapable of being happy; for, though he loved himself above all the world, and believed himself to be the wisest man and the best Soldier of the nation, and had places and preferments proportionable to very great merit (when, in truth, he had been liberally rewarded for all the services he had done, or could ever do, when he was Knighted;[1]) yet, with that favourable opinion of himself, he had so great an undervaluing of all other men, that he was more grieved and afflicted at any good fortune, or prefer- ment which other men attained to, than delighted with any promotion that befel himself; though considering his great infirmities, his weakness, and his vanity, which were not concealed, he had a greater proportion of good fortune than any man of that time. They who had known him throughout the whole course of his life, did believe his too good success in the world, together with the pride and vanity that he contracted from that success, so changed and corrupted his nature, that there remained in him nothing of that ingenuity, modesty, or generosity which made him liked and beloved in his younger time.

He was born a younger Brother of a very good family in the West, where his Father was owner of a very fair estate,[2] and a good interest and reputation, and lived with more splendour than his neighbours of his own rank, which caused some breach and waste in his estate; so that, having many younger sons, he gave them good education, and left them only moderate annuities to support their pretences in the world. This gentleman was the youngest of five or six sons, and being but a boy at the death of his Father, was left under the tuition of his mother, who was a wise woman, and took care of his breeding, and sent him to the University of Oxford, where he spent two or three years as well or better than gentlemen of that age usually do;[3] and then his inclinations carried him to London, which was the scene upon which active men first shewed themselves. As he was of a very good extraction by his Father, so he was by his mother allied to two good families, which at that time made some eclat in the Court, the Jermyns and the Killigrews, who were both possessed of very fair fortunes in their several countries; and by which, together with very good natural faculties, they endeavoured to promote themselves in the Court, and were in very good estimation there, and infected all their allies with an appetite to plant in that climate.

This gentleman chose first to see foreign armies abroad, as two of his Brothers had done before; and so going first into the Low-Countries, he chose to go into Germany with General Morgan when he possessed himself of Stade, where he had some command, but his health not agreeing with that climate, he removed into France, and having spent some time there, returned into England, and renewed his old inclinations and applications to the Court; but finding the ascents there not made with that expedition as they have been since, and being in his nature a little unsteady and irresolute, resolved to apply himself to such a course of life as might fit him for business, and so intitle him to make other pretences in the Court than to be a mere courtier, and with this resolution he made another journey into France, to make himself perfect in that language; and from thence made a journey into Spain, and thereby obtained a competency in that tongue, and with these faculties and qualifications he returned into England to prosecute his pretences in the Court. He was at this time generally beloved, and was always found in the best company, where he was very acceptable, being a man of good parts, and better bred, having seen more of the world, than most other men of that time, and being free from any lewd and scandalous vices; and in this state was well known in the Town and in the Court.

And an occasion falling out, in which the King thought it necessary to send an Envoy to the Court of Sweden,[4] he was made choice of, and performed his employment with approbation, and was shortly after rewarded with a place of attendance about the Queen, in the office of Gentleman Sewer, which was a relation the modesty of that time thought a very good preferment, and to him it was the more valuable, because his family and kindred were very powerful on that side of the House, and the greatest favours past by the Queen's mediation or approbation. But the troubles coming on, he easily got a dispensation for his attendance at Court, and engaged himself in the first levies, and having the reputation of knowing somewhat of war, which few young men could then pretend to, he commanded the Earl of Holland's own Troop, he being then General of the Horse and particularly kind to this gentleman. That war was quickly ended, but it produced another which lasted too long, in the beginning whereof he grew to be a Major of Horse, and being of the Court as well as the Camp, and a man generally esteemed, he was embarked in some intrigues with his friends at Court, which being ill-founded, and having success accordingly, he was forced to leave the Kingdom, and upon his return was committed to the Tower by the Parliament, as a man disaffected to their proceedings, which made him more known, and gave him more credit, without any further inconvenience to him. So when the King withdrew to York, and sent the Marquis of Hertford with a commission to secure the Western parts, he, with the other principal Gentleman of those counties, attended the Marquis to assist him in the command of an Army; Sir Ralph Hopton and he being looked upon as men of the greatest experience in martial affairs, which most of the rest were absolutely without, and so were designed to commands accordingly.

The first attempt in the West being quickly blasted, and the Marquis withdrawing himself into Wales, and from thence to the King at Oxford, he had the good fortune in good company to go into Cornwall, where he found the principal persons of quality and interest ready to receive them with open arms, and to wed the King's interest; and so uniting themselves together, as good friends and good subjects, after two or three prosperous encounters with the enemy, they became of most credit in that county, having at Liskard, and other places given several defeats to the enemy, and their whole forces; in which actions this gentleman had a good part, there being none amongst them who had a commission to command in chief, but carried on the war by mutual consent, and by assigning such parts to particular persons as was jointly thought fit. The news of this being brought to the King by the Lord Mohun, who pretended to be purposely sent to give his Majesty an account thereof, whereas in truth (as was known afterwards) he had left Cornwall before the time of that defeat, with a purpose to keep himself from being engaged on either side in the country, and to betake himself to the Parliament; but the news of that action over-taking him as he came through Devonshire, and then hearing of the battle of Edge-hill, and his Majesty's march towards London, he found the King at Colebrook upon his retreat from Brentford, and pretended to be sent as well to desire commissions for the carrying on the war there, as to inform his Majesty of the success they had had, and that his return was hourly expected, before which they would not know how to proceed. That Lord knew very well how to make a large relation, and though he had scarce ever seen those persons who were engaged for the King in Cornwall, much less had engaged himself with them, except by promises, and was fallen into their jealousy by not having performed those promises, he was still too near the places where all the actions had been, to be ignorant of what had passed, and so was very particular in all his relations, insomuch as it was really believed he had been present in all the actions, and he proposed such commissions for the command of the forces which were or should be raised, that his Majesty's service might proceed with the best success, which was of absolute necessity to be done; for the Marquis of Hertford had invested no body with his commission to command in chief, which the King knew not till then. The dispatch would not bear delay, and it was made upon very short deliberation, which succeeded better than reasonably could be expected. The Lord, who pretended to be the messenger, was utterly unknown, being a very young man, only that all men knew he had a good fortune in that country and was well allied; and the zeal he now professed made it thought fit to qualify him with some trust.

Sir Ralph Hopton was known to have a very great interest in the county of Somerset, where he had a noble fortune, and in all respects was believed to be qualified for the greatest trust. Sir John Berkley had many very good friends at Court, and was believed to be a good Officer, and Colonel Ashburnham, who was likewise there, had a Brother in very good credit with the King, so that without any consideration of the place where they were, or of the persons by whose interest all had been done, a commission was immediately granted to the Lord Mohun, Sir Ralph Hopton, Colonel Ashburnham and Sir John Berkley, or to any three of them, to command those forces, and to grant any commissions for the raising more; and in sum, to execute the office of a General; and with this commission the Lord Mohun made all the haste he could possibly back into Cornwall, and then joined himself to the rest, who, upon less authority, would not have joined with him upon any thing.

The persons whose interest and reputation had the whole influence upon Cornwall, was Sir Bevill Greenville, Arundel of Trerice with his two Sons, Sir Nicholas Slanning, who was Governor of Pendennis, the only garrison in that county, and Trevanian with his Son, who had married the Daughter of Arundel, all who were Deputy Lieutenants, Parliament Men, and of the greatest estates and reputation in the country; these gentlemen had received and entertained the other who fled thither, and joined themselves to them for the support and maintenance of the King's authority, against those who came armed with commissions from the Parliament to suppress it, and having upon the matter, by their own credit, and at their own expence, suppressed all those who declared for the Parliament, for which they stood likewise accused in Parliament as persons guilty of high Treason, they now found themselves upon the Lord Mohun's coming, and upon the view of the commission he brought, without any kind of authority over the men they had raised, and that they were as all the rest, entirely subject to the commands of those four Commissioners; one whereof, though of their own country and of quality above them, had yet much less reputation and credit there, than the meanest of them; and the other three, absolute strangers and unknown in the country; two of them without any estate or fortune in any other place; all which would quickly have made such a commission very ineffectual, if it had not met with persons wholly divested of any ambition but to serve the King, or of private interest but to promote the public. And so without any expostulation or murmur, they all submitted to the command of the Commissioners, who again were so wise (three of them being very innocent and utterly unknowing how it came to be procured) as to exercise their authority in such a manner, that nothing was done without their advice and approbation, so that they all seemed to be equal sharers in the same command; and in this union, and by their good discipline, and sober behaviour towards the country, they prospered so much that they drew together a good body of foot, and three or four hundred horse, with a train of artillery.

And the Parliament having sent down the Earl of Stamford with an army much superior in horse, foot, and cannon, to reduce that county to their obedience, and to take the Castle of Pendennis, they adventured with their little army to meet him at the borders of their country; and when the Earl was encamped on the top of a hill, and whilst he had sent his horse to get behind them and to cut off their retreat, they marched in four bodies, in the four steep and narrow ways which led up to the hill, and executed it with so much order and courage, that they all got to the top of the hill together, beat them out of their trenches, killed all who resisted, and took the most of the rest prisoners, with all their baggage and ordnance; the Earl himself with a few servants making his escape in the beginning of the action. This so complete a victory reduced that whole country to the King's obedience, and the Commanders sent his Majesty word, that if they might have a supply of horse sent to join with them in Somersetshire, where the enemy was strong, they would be ready to march with their army as his Majesty should direct; whereupon the Marquis of Hertford was again sent with a competent strength of Horse, and some few Foot to receive that army, and therewith to make himself master of the West, the Parliament at the same time sending down Sir William Waller with a good body to preserve their interest. The very notable encounters in that march, and the great actions which followed it, are fit to be remembered at large for the honour of many persons in a more proper discourse.

This gentleman,[5] the very first night the forces joined, contrived how he might get out of that company where he was to have so many superiors, and proposed to return back into Devonshire, to shut up the Earl of Stamford in Exeter untill he could raise strength enough to besiege him, and by that means to prevent the raising a greater body of men both in that County and in Cornwall, which the Parliament would be very well able to do, if the City of Exeter were entirely free. The proposition was very agreeable to the general wish, for there was reason to apprehend the inconvenience of such levies, and every body was very willing to spare him to the service, being a man extremely uneasy to his superiors and his equals; and so he returned with such a small body of Horse and Foot as could be well spared, amongst which he had the good fortune to have some very good Officers, and a conjunction with persons in the Country of very good reputation; and so he blocked up Exeter at such a distance as was inconvenient to them, and exposed himself and his soldiers to small danger or difficulty; and in this posture he remained for the space of five or six months, until Prince Maurice marched thither, after the taking of Bristol, with such a strength as easily reduced the City of Exeter, where he remained Governor with such a garrison as was sufficient.

From this time he either changed, or discovered his nature, for he never afterwards appeared the same man he had formerly been, but grew to such an imperiousness in command, and so much vanity in extolling himself, that all men found it very hard to live with him, who were not very much below him, and towards those he lived very agreeably, for he was at the mercy of every body who would take the pains to flatter him, and in this very easy state of government, where he had what money he pleased, and lived very generously, and had greater allowance so to do than any Officer who marched in the Army, he continued to the end of the war, having the supreme command of those two large Counties of Cornwall and Devonshire, without performing any considerable service in his own person, or lodging many nights out of his garrison; and though he did make two or three attempts upon the enemy, in which he had always with him a good strength, he always returned to his garrison without success or reputation, and in this posture he continued to the end of the war; a little before the conclusion whereof, and as soon as the enemy came within any distance of the town, which was better fortified than most places in England, and well supplied with provisions, he delivered all up, upon such conditions as were given of course in such cases; and shortly after, the war being ended, he repaired into France to the Queen, where he remained until the King was in the hands of the Army, and when the Officers seemed to pay him that respect, that many men believed he would have preserved himself and his interest by the assistance of his enemies, which he could not do by the help of his friends; and that the Army which had subdued all his forces, would do all for him which he could have wished from his own Army, if it had prevailed, the chief Officers of that Army having no possibility to have supported themselves in their contests with, and rebellion against the Parliament, but by having the King in their hands, and making such professions, and paying such respects to them as made almost the whole kingdom believe, that their intentions were very real towards him, and to restore the Kingdom to its ancient happiness.

This gentleman had been very happy if he had been either qualified to do business, or composed to be quiet without meddling in any; but he was of so unhappy a constitution as that he had a very perplexed understanding, and a more perplexed delivery and expression, and yet believed he was fit for the greatest transactions; and he was of so restless a nature that he could never be quiet in a good condition, nor patient in a bad; and therefore as soon as the news came to Paris of the King's marching in the head of the Army, he began to think of having a good part in the action, and made offer of his service to the Queen, assuring her that he had very great interest in the principal Officers of the Army, telling many particular discourses to her that he had held with them when he delivered up Exeter, not without some insinuation as if he believed the good affection the army now shewed towards the King, was the result of his advice to them; and he made now no question but that by his interest in them, he should easily get admittance to the King, and thereby be able to do him very notable service. There was one argument (which hath been the true cause of most of his promotions) that prevailed more with the Queen, and those about her, whose advice she most followed, than any of his insinuations; which was, that they were all so weary of him, and of his chagrin humour, that they were willing to embrace any motion to be rid of him; and so he went into England with as full a recommendation from the Queen, as she could have given to a man of whom she thought very well.

The King had very little knowledge of him, and as little inclination to him, but he found himself not unwelcome to the Officers of the army, who well knew his foible, and so readily admitted him to attend the King, which licence they gave to very few, and therefore his Majesty found it necessary to trust and employ him, having no suspicion of his want of integrity, in which point he was not to be suspected. When the Officers of the army had made all the use they meant to do of the King, and subdued all those who opposed them, and so treated his Majesty with less respect than they had formerly done, so that he thought it necessary to make an escape from the army, he took only this Gentleman and John Ashburnham, the latter of whom he had intrusted to provide a Ship for him, to transport him beyond the Seas; but, by what accident was not known, there was no Ship ready, whereupon the King went to Tichfield, the Earl of Southampton's House in the new Forest, not far distant from the Sea, which was inhabited by the Old Countess of Southampton, the Earl her Son being then at a house of his own far distant from thence. When the King had a little refreshed himself there, it was resolved very unreasonably to send to Hammond, then Governor of the Isle of Wight, of whom there was a better opinion entertained than he any ways deserved,[6] and to try whether he might be trusted so far as that the King might lie concealed within his Government, until he could take further resolutions; and the two persons before named were sent to confer with him, with an express command from the King that they should not let him know where he was, except he gave them his word to be faithful. They found the person very civil to them, but in no degree disposed to pass his word, or to enter into any treaty with them, but desired to know where his Majesty was, and fatally prevailed with them to carry him with them to the King, and then there was no avoiding it, but that his Majesty must go into the Isle of Wight, where he afterwards remained, under that restraint which is too well known, which continued to his death. These two persons lay ever under great reproaches for their ill conduct of that so precious affair, which requires an ample enlargement in a more proper place. Shortly after, this Gentleman was forbid any farther access to the King, and so he returned again into France to be near the Queen, where the Prince then likewise was.

The Duke of York, and the rest of the King's Children, were under the charge of the Earl of Northumberland, at his house at Sion, and afterwards were removed to St. James's, from whence he found means to make an escape, and a small vessel being provided for him, he transported himself into Holland, where he was kindly received by the Prince of Orange and the Princess Royal his Sister, and from thence gave an account of himself to the Queen his Mother and to the Prince his Brother. And his Royal Highness had not been long there before the revolt of the Fleet, under the command of the Earl of Warwick,[7] to their obedience to the King, and, sending their chief Officers on shore, they hoist sail, and steered for Holland, declaring that they would find out their Admiral, meaning the Duke of York, who was designed by his Father for that office, as soon as he should be of age. The news of this, and some other revolutions in England, in which the Earl of Holland and many other persons of honour were engaged, together with the great preparations in Scotland under the command of Duke Hamilton, made it counsellable for the Prince to leave Paris, and to bring himself to Calais, from whence likewise he was transported to the Brill in Holland, where the Ships of the Royal Navy were then present, and where he found the Duke his Brother. Before the Prince of Wales removed from Paris, and upon the first news of the Fleet, the Queen thought it necessary that some person of discretion should be sent into Holland to attend the person of the Duke, who had no other servants about him but those who had contributed to his escape, and merited that trust thereby; and the principal of those, and who upon the matter had alone performed that service, though he deserved very well by it, was of so hot and restless a head, that he was not to be relied upon,[8] being a man of wit and great insinuation, and as ready to embark the Duke in any design, in which he himself might probably receive advantage by being nearest to him, how much soever it might reflect to the prejudice of the King or the Prince. The Queen thought it necessary to send some person of a superior condition, and with the authority of a Governor about the Duke, and so sent Sir John Berkley, under whom the gentleman who was with the Duke had served as an inferior Officer, and so could make no scruple to obey him, and he himself well knew that he could supply that place during the absence of the Lord Byron, who had before been made Governor to his Royal Highness by the King, and was at that time in Ireland in his Majesty's service. Having got this relation to the Duke, he seemed satisfied for some time, having the convenience of living plentifully, and being superior to all those who were related to the Duke, towards whom he carried himself always very imperiously.

When the Lord Byron returned out of Ireland, and came to attend upon the person of the Duke in his place of Governor, Sir John, who could in no degree indure to be inferior to any man, withdrew from his attendance, and by degrees insinuated to him that it was time for him to be without a Governor, which the Duke was willing enough to hearken to, and the Queen being likewise wrought upon to consent, which seemed to be the more reasonable, because it was thought fit that the Duke should go into the Campaign to learn the art of war, under the care of Marshall Turenne, the Lord Byron was very willing to lay down his title of Governor at the Duke's feet, and to attend him in any qualification he thought reasonable, and so he had the reputation, as there was good reason, of being chief of his servants, which took away all joy from the other, who yet attended upon his Highness a Campaign or two, and then the Lord Byron died,[9] which put him again into the chiefest and first relation, and he gave himself the title of Intendant of the affairs of his Royal Highness. He had hitherto never made himself acceptable to the Duke, nor loved by any of his fellow servants; his pride, and superciliousness was such, and his vanity so great in magnifying himself, and extolling his own abilities in war, that when he came out of the field, he always entertained those with whom he conversed, with stories, how much Marshall Turenne governed himself by his advice, and that such, and such actions had never been undertaken, but by his direction; and he was happy in the good opinion he had of himself, in which no body concurred with him. He was very importunate with the King to make him a Privy Counseller and Master of the Wards, to which he pretended a promise from the late King, which had no foundation of truth, and if it had, there was no use of such an Officer whilst his Majesty was abroad, and therefore the King expressly refused to bestow it upon him or to make him of his Council, there being so many persons about him of superior quality, and who could in all respects more reasonably pretend to that honour; but this refusal deprived him of all patience, and made him break friendship with the only friend he had, because he would not assist him in those unreasonable pretences, and dissuaded him from pursuing them. From this time he endeavoured to make himself more gracious to the Duke, and the King being gone out of France into Germany, and the Duke spending the winter always with the Queen his Mother, who was always very gracious to Sir John, he found means to improve his credit very much with his Master, and put such persons about him of his own kindred and family, as would be disposed of by him, and made the condition of all his other servants very uneasy to them, and he so behaved himself that the King was in no degree satisfied with him.

After Cromwell's Treaty with France, the Duke found it necessary to leave France, and to retire to the King his Brother into Flanders, where, shortly after his arrival at Bruges, the King was persuaded by the Lord of Bristol and Mr. Bennett, who was the Secretary to the Duke, to remove Sir John Berkley from his attendance upon his Brother, as a person who infused jealousies into him of his Majesty's kindness, which was very intire to his Royal Highness.

Those who were about the King, and had as much or more credit with him than either of the other two,[10] would have been very glad to have diverted the King from that resolution, not out of kindness to the Knight, or opinion of his innocence, but they thought it would do him too much honour to make him thought so considerable, as if his presence could have had that influence; but the King had passed his word to the other two, and resolved to execute it, though the Duke appeared very much troubled at it; and so Sir John left the Court, and the Duke within three days afterwards (after he had first taken away his Seal, and discarded Mr. Bennett from his service) early in a morning left Bruges, and went into Zealand, and from thence to Breda, where he found Sir John Berkley, and from whence he writ to the King with great complaint of the treatment he had received, and that his servants should be removed from him without any fault committed by them. It was not a good conjuncture, when the Crown had so many enemies and so few friends, that there should appear any disunion between the King and his Brother, who was Heir Apparent to the Crown, and therefore his Majesty invited his Brother with great kindness to return to him, with permission that the other might likewise attend him. The Duke had not been long there, when he prevailed with his Majesty to create Sir John Berkley a Baron,[11] which all men wondered at, he having no pretence to any one acre of land in the world, nor being worth the cloaths he wore, and this extraordinary favour, which all the world wondered at, served only to whet his appetite, and for an argument to the King to confer an estate, because he had conferred an honour upon him.

From the hour of the King's coming into England, the new Lord set his heart upon nothing but getting money for himself by all the ways imaginable, and the Duke, who by this time was grown very weary of him, was yet willing to interceed for him to the King, and suffered him to be his own carver, and take what he would to himself out of his revenue; and appeared very kind to him in his treaty of Marriage, by which he obtained a young Widow, Daughter to an Alderman,[12] with whom he had a considerable fortune. When the Office of the President of Connaught in the Kingdom of Ireland became void by the death of the Earl of Montrath, he became a suiter for it, and the Duke solicited it, and the King bestowed it upon him for no other reason, but to be rid of him, he having professed that he meant to reside in the execution of that Office in that Kingdom, which he ought to have done, and in order thereunto carried his wife into Ireland, with which the Court was very well pleased; but he stayed no longer there than to let his Office to farm for a good yearly rent, and so returned again to Court the better prepared to make new suits, his importunity being in no degree allayed by any thing he had received, as if his high merit had yet received no recompence. Nor was he in truth in any degree delighted with what he got, out of the envy he had to see others obtain that which he thought himself fitter for.

He loved so much to be flattered, that he was at the mercy of any man who would attack him that way, and he paid liberally in the same kind, and was a very great flatterer himself, but of no body so much as of himself. He never loved his equals, and always hated his superiors, and was still governed by his inferiors; he had a very indifferent understanding, and a very obscure and troubled expression in debate, but inveighed against any thing that was concluded, and always believed himself the wisest man of the time, and took great pleasure in censuring the weakness and oversights in the time of King James, and of the Counsellers which governed then, of whom, and the business, he never understood any thing. He was full of pride, and not without courage, and would well enough have discharged the office of a soldier, if he had known how to have obeyed. Yet he valued himself in that profession, as if he had been Lieutenant General to Julius Caesar; but yet he never executed any design in the command he had with tolerable sufficiency, or with any success. Yet he had got a habit of telling stories of his own actions, as if he had performed miracles, and sustained the war in England by his own virtue, without ever receiving an affront from the enemy; and he had so accustomed himself to those discourses, that he had brought himself to believe all that he had reported. He had no friends who heartily esteemed him, and was the only person alive who compassed all that he set his heart upon, purely by his own ambition, without any merit, or ever having done any notable thing, but by a perpetual restlessness, and unquietness in himself, and being uneasy to every body else; or by affecting somewhat which other pretenders found not friends to keep them to, or that his friends did therefore help him to, to cross those pretenders. If he loved any body it was those whom he had known a very little while, and who had purchased his affection at the price of much application, and very much flattery; and if he had any friends, they were likewise such who had known him very little, or else such who loved nobody else. All men of parts who ever had a good opinion of him retired from it quickly, and either threw him quite off, or lived with a dry formality with him; only one, who was a worthy person indeed (Sir Hugh Pollard,[13] Comptroller of his Majesty's House) continued kind to him till his death; and being his cousin-german, and having spent the greatest part of his time in his company, believed he was to pay that penance for the error of his judgment; besides, his own longing disposition made him less acquainted with the improvement of his indiscretions than other men were; besides that he was much warier in his discourse to him, than to those he knew less, and many things that he said to him the other believed to proceed from his friendship in communication, and not from the malignity of his nature.

He seems to enjoy a very good health, yet a man may reasonably think that the passions of his mind, being very much stifled within himself, may work upon the temper of his body, and that he may die of an apoplexy; but it may be more reasonably conjectured, that they may have no influence upon his health, but work upon themselves, and then he may live to a great age, under so great a decay of his natural faculties, that he may be a strong man many years after the expiration of the parts of his mind, and after a full decay of all pretences to understanding his memory will decay apace, but his talking will leave him last.

Henry Jermyn, 1st Earl of St Albans in Garter
robes. Painted by Lely.

HENRY JERMYN
LATER
EARL OF ST. ALBANS

The reasons for this identification are set out in the Introduction (pp. 4–7) where such passages as require annotation
are discussed.

HE WAS A MAN BRED FROM HIS CRADLE IN THE COURT, AND
had no other business in the world than to be a good
Courtier; in the arts whereof he succeeded so well, that he
may well be reckoned in the number of the finest gentlemen
of the time; and, though his parts of nature were very mean,
and never improved by industry, yet, passing his time always
in good company, and well acquainted with what was done
in all businesses, he would speak well and reasonably to any
purpose. He was in his nature so very civil, that no man was
more easily lived with, except his interest was concerned; and
in that he was so tenacious, that he observed no rules of
courtesy, reason, or justice; in all other matters he offended
nobody: but then his interest could never be discerned but by
his importunity, being very ready, for his profit, to engage
himself in any undertaking where he had credit, in which he
neither considered the justice of the suit, or the honour of the
person with whom he desired to prevail; but except it was for
his profit, he never troubled himself heartily in any man's
pretences, what relation or merit soever the party had towards
him. He practised such a kind of civility, and had such a
mean in making professions, that they were oftentimes mis-

taken for friendship, which he never meant, or was guilty of to any man; but did really believe that his kind words and exercise of courtesy deserved the utmost service they could possibly do him. He was rather a lover of mankind than of any particular person, and would have done no man any harm except he could get by it, and then he cared not what he did, and thought no man ought to take it ill. He was not mischievous in his nature or inclinations, yet did more mischief than any man of the age he lived in, being the occasion of more prejudice to the King and to the Crown than any man of his condition ever was, and took more pains to lessen the King's reputation, and to make his person undervalued, than any other man did; and all this without the least purpose of infidelity, or desire of abating his prerogative, which he wished should be as high as any King's ever was, and desired only that they might prevail over it over whom he could prevail, and in that regard he cared not how low his reputation came to be.

He was in his nature very covetous and tenacious, liberal in no degree, and denied all men but himself, and to himself was very indulgent, especially in his diet, which was magnificent enough, and his table was free to all men; but none so welcome to it as gamesters, all his delight and expence was in play, which was the spunge that sucked in, and the gulph that swallowed up all he could get. His ambition was illimited, that no Prince hath so much to give as he thought he had deserved; and after he had lived above forty years at the expence of the Crown, and spent more than any body else had got, he thought the Court still in his debt, and that his having lived in it so many years, had merited much more than he had ever received from it. If he were ever affected with melancholy, it was in considering what religion to be of, when that which he professed was so much discountenanced that he was almost weary of it; yet few men so often upon their knees, or so much desired to be thought a good Protestant by all the parties which professed that Faith, and could willingly comply with all of them, and yet took time of the Roman Catholics to be better informed.

He was a great flatterer of those who were above him, and a great dissembler to his equals and inferiors, and of all vices he was least guilty of pride, except in preferring himself before all men, which they could never know; and he was of a temper and constitution that exceedingly contributed to his happiness; for though he loved nobody, he believed every body loved him, which was a great argument of having the master wit: he never underwent any other mortification than seeing men preferred whom he did not care for, or other men obtain that which he wished to have for himself. In the greatest miseries of the Kingdom, and whilst the greatest and the best men were exercised with all kinds of adversity, he enjoyed the greatest plenty and pomp; and the King no sooner came home but he believed his merit in being banished was greater than any man's sufferings could pretend to. He loves his country, as it is a good place to be a great man in, but would give it up to be made greater any where else; in a word, he would be a very extraordinary man, if he were endowed with any kind of sincerity, and if he dies without some very signal calamity, he may well be looked upon as a man of rare felicity.

Henry Bennet, 1st Earl of Arlington, after Lely.

Sir Henry Bennet

LATER
EARL OF ARLINGTON

H E WAS A GREAT INSTANCE HOW MUCH FORTUNE CAN DO towards the raising a man without any help of his own; for being without money, without friends, without industry, or any one notable virtue, or the reputation of having any, he mounted up to office and honour, and the highest trust in business, without any experience in it, or capacity of understanding it; and very few men have ever ascended to such a height, *per saltum*,[1] without climbing by steps.

He was a younger brother of a broken and decayed family, by the vice and corruption of the person who raised it, and fell scandalously after a short prosperity.[2] He was sent to the University,[3] where he had a competent support by the bounty of the founder; and his parts of nature were such as were very capable of improvement by moderate industry, had not he valued them too high to administer any help of that kind. He had the opportunity to be recommended to a great person of business and fancy,[4] who took him into his service, and esteemed him much the more because he found his nature and humour very like his own, and believed he had somewhat extraordinary in him, because he seemed to think so himself. He had address enough to make himself acceptable to any man who loved to hear himself commended and admired, and he could perform that part with dexterity enough. Though he got nothing of experience in business by this relation, he got both credit and money to carry him into

France, and from thence into Italy, in a dependence upon a person who knew much and talked much, under whose protection he staid some months in Rome.[5] He profited very well in understanding the languages of the places where he lived, and made himself a good master in the French tongue; and by his address made himself so gracious to the Queen and her Court, where he was allied to some persons[6] who had much credit and interest there, that he was preferred by the Queen to be near the person of the Duke of York, by which he became likewise known to the King.

His chief talent was being pleasant, and good company amongst those who were his superiors; amongst his equals and inferiors his insolence was intolerable. He met there with one of his own humour, of his own pride, and of his own ambition, to whom though he was superior to him in parts, the other was superior in interest as well as in quality,[7] which made him weary of that station, and thereupon he became a spy upon his master, and observed all that was said or done, and made the worst interpretation of all that it could bear; and if the King had not had a nature superior to all temptations, he had then kindled a jealousy between the two brothers, and did go so far towards it that the Duke put him out of his service, and himself for sometime left the Court, but soon after returned. His friends prevailed with the King to send him into Spain as an Envoy,[8] when he could be in no degree useful to his Majesty's service in that Court, merely to put the better countenance upon the other disgrace. He rendered himself very acceptable in that Court by making a show of being inclined to that Religion, and never pressing any thing that was uneasy to them.

Whilst the King was at Brussels, and coldly treated, there was an Irish Jesuit, one Peter Talbot,[9] who had great credit with Don Alonzo de Cardenas, and held a correspondence with the Levelling Party in England, very much to his Majesty's prejudice, towards whom he lived with great insolence, and printed a scandalous book or two in English against the Church of England, in which he had many reflections of contempt, which reflected upon his Majesty and his Councils. Upon which the King complained of him to those Ministers, but Don Alonzo supported him; yet the Superiors of his Order paid that respect to his Majesty, that they would not suffer him to stay at Brussels, which he contested with the Superior for some time; and shortly after, with the countenance of Don Alonzo, he transported himself into England, and found so much countenance there, that when the Treaty was like to be between France and Spain, he was employed by Cromwell into Spain in hope to break that Treaty; and promised that he would so prevail in Spain, by the credit that Don Alonzo had given him there, that the King should not be suffered to stay longer in Flanders. Of all which his Majesty having received full and clear information from England, he sent order to his Envoy at Madrid that he should desire the King and Don Louis de Haro, that he might not be admitted to come thither; that being his Majesty's own subject, and having behaved himself so very ill towards him, his Majesty expected, that upon this representation of his, he should not receive any countenance there; but the Envoy was so far from observing this order from his Majesty, that he entered into a great familiarity and friendship with Talbot, and consulted with him in all things, for which he made no other excuse than that he found it necessary, and that he had much more credit there than he had; which disobedience and presumption would have been very penal, nor would at any time have been ventured upon by any other man than of his spirit.

When the King came to Fontarabia, upon the close of the Treaty, the Envoy met him there, and, by the advantage of having the language, quickly got all the business into his hands; by the advantage whereof he treated those of the King's Council, who waited upon his Majesty,[10] with such insolence, that they returned very unsatisfied with him; but he himself went back to Madrid, getting as much money from the King, out of that Ayuda de Costa which the King of Spain presented his Majesty with, as he thought fit to require, with which he was not at all modest, and got more for himself than the King was able to bestow upon all the servants who attended him, and upon all those who remained at Brussels in expectation of his return.

As soon as the King returned into England, he took upon him to make a Treaty with Spain according to his own discretion; and without having any Letters of Revocation, or so much as desiring them by interposition of either of the Secretaries of State, he procured, by a private motion of a Groom of the Bedchamber,[11] leave from the King to return; and as the Spaniard had liberally supported him from the time of his coming thither, so they presented him very bountifully at his departure, and continued an allowance to him long after, under the notion of continuing his Dispense; all which enabled him to make his journey into England in a better equipage, and with more grandeur, than any foreign Minister had ever returned. The King received him with great kindness, as a man whose company he always liked; and he had not been long at Court before he prevailed with his Majesty to bestow the place of Keeper of his Privy Purse upon him, though his Majesty had promised that office to a nobleman who had done his Father very signal service, and for it was very particularly recommended to him by his Majesty, and from his death had constantly waited upon his Majesty at a great expence to the time of his return, and then returned with his Majesty, in full confidence and assurance of being possessed of that place.[12]

Though he was much now at his ease, and with reference to his faculties the most commodiously advanced, his ambition could not be quiet without prevailing by new importunities with the King, to remove an old faithful servant,[13] who had served the Crown in great trust for the space of little less than fifty years, had suffered banishment with the King, and returned with him; and because it would be a thing of too ill a fame to dismiss a servant of such fidelity, and so generally esteemed, without a good recompence, his Majesty himself was content to bestow upon him near the value of twenty

thousand pounds, and so made room for this new Minister of
State; who, as he could pretend to know nothing of England,
so he was in truth very ignorant in the affairs of any other
country, save that he understood the languages, having spent
his time wholly in conversation and romances, without ever
having read one serious writer, or any important Treaty
between any Princes; yet he quickly appeared to think better
of himself than of any who had been before him, or who
lived with him. Upon the King's desire he had been recommended by a Person from whom he deserved it not,[14] to
be chosen a Member of the House of Commons,[15] where all
the King's business had been carried on with as much success
as could be desired or wished; but he had not sat there many
days before he believed he understood the interest of England,
and the nature and humour of the Nation, at least as well as
any man; and, though he had no talent in speaking, he made
all the haste he could to ingratiate himself with those who he
found busy and pragmatical in the House, by which he
judged their interest; these men he caressed by offering them
to do them all services in the Court, and to recommend them
to the King, which he did too unhappily, making such partial
and unjust representations both of the transactions of the
House, and the persons who were most active in them, as
was most agreeable to his fancy, which could not in any
tolerable degree make a judgment of the one or of the other;
but by this means he made cabals and factions, by which the
measures which were before taken were quite broken, and
sober men discouraged from pursuing the public service with
that zeal and ardency they had formerly used, finding, as they
thought, very ill measures taken for the carrying on the
King's service; and his representations, with the concurrence
of some others, who having much better parts, had the same
end with him against particular persons, prevailed so far that
there was a visible alteration in all the King's affairs from his
first coming into that House, which was very shortly after
his coming to the Kingdom, and they who had before most
credit with his Majesty, grew by degrees to lose it in all

things wherein he appeared to be of another judgment.

No man contributed more to the war with Holland, in the debate whereof, or indeed in any other point of importance, though he never offered to give or answer any reasons; he found opportunity in private whispers, and between jest and earnest to undervalue what was said contrary to his inclinations, and the men who said it, turning the gravest and most substantial discourses into ridicule, which was a wit much in fashion; and never made conscience to discover and disclose whatsoever was said in Council of what nature soever, and under all the obligations of secrecy, if thereby he might bring prejudice to those to whom out of pure envy he wished not well. He used all his skill and credit with the King to lessen the credit of all those who had had any trust from his Father, and long experience in affairs, declaring them to be only men of form, and of narrow comprehensions, and who guided themselves by obsolete rules of law and conscience, which were not now a good standard to govern the State by. He never made a noble friendship, nor ever loved a man of a clear fame and reputation, except he was of such an inferior quality, as would absolutely make him at his disposal.

He loves money immoderately, and would get it by all means imaginable, but his pride, and vanity, and ambition lead him into such a prodigious expence, that his gains must exceed all reasonable computation if he grows very rich, which he does impatiently desire to be. Justice was never otherwise considered or mentioned by him, but as it gave him occasion and opportunity to enveigh against the law, as a composition of nonsense, and not to be endured or submitted to by generous minds; and to express his malice and bitterness towards the Lawyers, who are a people he envies, hates, and contemns as though[16] all his passions and affections are engaged and involved in such contradictions; and yet he is not of those who fancy any other form or model of justice, otherwise than that he admires France, and thinks fit that all Kings and Princes should do whatsoever they have a mind to do without control, and that all that other men have, should be at their disposal. If he hath any inclinations in Religion, they are to the Church of Rome, being a people with whom he hath most conversed, and to whom he hath too much undervalued the Protestant Religion (which he never understood) to seem now to have any reverence for it, but surely he is without affection to, at least reverence for, any religion, and entertains discourse of it, as a field wide and large for all skirmishes of wit. In a word he is the first man that ever aimed to be great in Government without the least pretence of caring for religion or of love to justice, and if his days end in prosperity he will be a rare example.

NOTES

DIGBY

1 More probably in England in 1610/1611. See M. F. Keeler *The Long Parliament, a biographical study of its members* (Philadelphia 1954).

2 John Digby, first Earl of Bristol (1580–1653), diplomatist and statesman. For his career see *D.N.B.* The successful rivalry of Buckingham, to whom the Hyde family were clients, kept him out of the offices to which his abilities and services might have been thought to entitle him. Clarendon's attitude in this passage expresses a judicious compromise with his own past.

3 Magdalen College, where he was the pupil of Peter Heylyn, Laud's henchman and first biographer.

4 Sherborne Castle, Dorset. The new house had been built in the grounds of the still surviving medieval fortress by Sir Walter Ralegh in 1594.

5 These letters were written in 1638–9 and published in 1651.

6 Will Crofts (? 1611–1677) later ennobled by Charles II during his exile, apparently in return for his undertaking the upbringing of the King's son by Lucy Walter, the future Duke of Monmouth. Crofts had no enviable reputation for courage. The circumstances of the quarrel with Digby are described in *C.S.P. Dom* 17 June 1634.

7 This criticism is supported by Shaftesbury in his *Autobiography*. For his speeches in 1640–1, see Rushworth *Historical Collections* III, 170–4, IV 30, 146, 170, 225 and S. R. Gardiner *History of England* ix, 277.

8 'If the land of Ida (*sc.* Crete) had born two men of such quality'. Virgil *Aeneid* xi, 285. Virgil in fact wrote 'duo'. 'Duos', though equally grammatical, does not scan.

9 On 10 June 1641. That very morning Henry Marten moved in the Commons that the House should send for him as a result of a violent scene on 8 June from which Digby had been lucky to escape without injury. See Gardiner *op. cit.* ix, 385–6.

10 The skirmish at Aldbourne Chase on 18 September 1643. The battle of Newbury was fought on the 20th.

11 The MS originally read '. . . and oblige the nuncio to quit . . .'. The expansion of the text is in Clarendon's own hand.

12 This sentence, ending with ' . . . the King his father', is lightly struck through in the MS.

13 Capel and Colepeper. This phrase 'the two lords . . .' is inserted in Clarendon's own hand.

14 Clarendon himself, as is made clear in the *Life*.

15 'imagination' inserted in Clarendon's hand and 'fancy' deleted.

16 Substituted by Clarendon for the original reading of 'Enemies'.

17 This passage about the Cardinal's letter to the old Prince of Condé has been extensively corrected in Clarendon's hand, clarifying and amplifying details but not altering the sense.

18 This concluding phrase is inserted in Clarendon's hand, followed by a cross and the note 'writ pa. 1 × 2', presumably a cross-reference to a MS which the copyist had been following.

19 Carte's *Life of Ormond* (iv, 569) is more charitable: 'The cardinal readily advanced him 10,000 pistoles . . . With this sum, and a full persuasion that the prince would come to Ireland when it was thought necessary, and that France would supply further sums of money for the forbearance of calling him from thence, Lord Digby returned to Ireland, and landed at Waterford on June 29th.'

20 The Fronde.

21 'You must live upon iron: beauty of plumage is besides the point.'

22 Digby was given the Garter in Paris in January 1653 and installed by proxy on 15 April 1661.

23 Mme de Châtillon.

24 Clarendon's rooted objection to the term 'Prime Minister', as being a French expression for a French thing, is no doubt responsible for this franglais.

25 'He failed however in daring great things.' Ovid *Metamorphoses* ii, 328.

26 The Civil Governor of the Spanish Netherlands.

27 Francis I (1629–58).

28 The close links between the House of Orange and the House of Stuart explain the hostility of De Witt's Republican government.

29 St. Ghislain is about thirty miles S.S.W. of Brussels.

30 Sir Edward Nicholas.

31 Lady Diana Digby.

32 *sic* in MS. ?Albi.

33 Clarendon.

34 'Now that you are converted, go and convert your brethren.'

SIR JOHN BERKELEY

1 At Berwick-on-Tweed, 27 July 1639.

2 At Bruton in Somerset.

3 Berkeley matriculated on 14 February 1623 from Queen's College, Oxford.

4 In January 1637.